7 Practices of Effective Ministry

7

PRACTICES
OF EFFECTIVE
MINISTRY

ANDY STANLEY
REGGIE JOINER
LANE JONES

Multnomah® Publishers *Sisters, Oregon*

7 PRACTICES OF EFFECTIVE MINISTRY
published by Multnomah Publishers, Inc.

© 2004 by North Point Ministries, Inc.
International Standard Book Number: 1-59052-373-3

Cover design by David Carlson Design
Cover images by Eric Rank/Photonica

Unless otherwise indicated, Scripture quotations are from:
The Holy Bible, New International Version © 1973, 1984 by International Bible Society, used by permission of Zondervan Publishing House.

Multnomah is a trademark of Multnomah Publishers, Inc.,
and is registered in the U.S. Patent and Trademark Office.
The colophon is a trademark of Multnomah Publishers, Inc.

Printed in the United States of America

For information:
MULTNOMAH PUBLISHERS, INC. • P.O. BOX 1720 • SISTERS, OREGON 97759

Library of Congress Cataloging-in-Publication Data

Joiner, Reggie.
    The 7 practices of effective ministry / Reggie Joiner, Lane Jones, Andy Stanley.
        p. cm.
    Includes bibliographical references.
    ISBN 1-59052-373-3
    1.   Pastoral theology.   I. Title: Seven practices of effective ministry. II Jones, Lane. III. Stanley, Andy. IV. Title.

    BV4011.3.J65 2004
    253—dc22

                                            2004007595

05 06 07 08 09 10—10 9 8 7 6 5 4

To the Leadership Team of North Point Community Church, with whom we have had the pleasure of living out these seven practices. Our prayer is that we always remain on the same page.

Julie Arnold
Rick Holliday
Reggie Joiner
Lane Jones
David McDaniel
Andy Stanley
Bill Willits

CONTENTS

Preface: A New Season 9

Part I
Getting in the Game: Ray's Story

1   The Best-Laid Plans 15

2   Throwing Strikes 23

3   Keeping Score 31

4   Getting on Base 35

5   Staying Focused 39

6   Teaching the Fundamentals 43

7   The Roar of the Crowd 49

8   Developing New Talent 53

9   Managing Your Way to Victory 57

Part II
Putting the 7 Practices to Work

Introduction: A Dilemma 63

10   PRACTICE #1: Clarify the Win 69
Define what is important at every level of the organization

11   PRACTICE #2: Think Steps, Not Programs 87
Before you start anything, make sure it takes you where you need to go

12   PRACTICE #3: Narrow the Focus 99
Do fewer things in order to make a greater impact

13   PRACTICE #4: Teach Less for More 119
Say only what you need to say to the people who need to hear it

14   PRACTICE #5: Listen to Outsiders 139
Focus on who you're trying to reach, not who you're trying to keep

15   PRACTICE #6: Replace Yourself 157
Learn to hand off what you do

16   PRACTICE #7: Work On It 173
Take time to evaluate your work—and to celebrate your wins

Epilogue: A Final Challenge 185

Notes 187

A NEW SEASON

Every Monday morning at 8:00, I sit down with our staff leadership team at North Point Community Church for a time of learning. These are valuable times. And honestly, these are often frustrating times. Frustrating because we are forced to look beyond where we are to where we could and should be as an organization.

These are the discussions that, in terms of programming, lead to new beginnings and untimely deaths.

The debate is unfiltered. At times it gets personal. We've all lost our cool at one time or another. I'm not always right. And there are mornings when it seems like we are wasting everybody's time.

But we continue to meet. We continue to harness our differences for the sake of synergy. Consequently, we continue to learn and grow together.

Over and over it is the seven practices described in this book that have enabled us to punch through the fog of information and emotion. It is our commitment to these seven guidelines that has enabled us to find clarity and make the tough calls. These seven principles provide the context for all of our discussions and decisions.

Dozens of wonderful books have been written for church leaders on how to increase attendance, develop programming, or disciple people. This is not one of those books.

The 7 *Practices of Effective Ministry* is not so much about what to *do* as it is about what to *ask*. This book will not tell you how to implement 'programs, but it will provide you with a new lens through which to evaluate your current programs and any you may be considering.

You will find no new strategy hidden in these pages. But as you embrace each of these seven practices, your ministry cannot help but become more strategic in everything it does.

PRACTICES, NOT PROGRAMS

The seven practices are just that—*practices*. These are not new program ideas. You don't have to be in church work long to discover that there are no one-size-fits-all programs. Ministry is more art than science, and our ever-changing culture makes it necessary to constantly evaluate, launch, and occasionally even kill programming.

The seven practices are designed to provide a template that will help you determine which programs to start, what to stop, and how to improve what's working. When implemented properly, these practices will energize every facet of your ministry.

So what are these seven practices?

1. *Clarify the Win.* It is impossible to know if you are making progress if you are not clear about your destination. This means examining each and every event and program and asking the question, When all is said and done, what is it we want to look back on and celebrate?

2. *Think Steps, Not Programs.* Your programs should take people somewhere, not simply fill up their time. Ask yourself, Where do we

want our people to be? What do we want them to become? Is our programming designed to take them there?

3. *Narrow the Focus.* Focus is the key to achieving excellence and making an impact. Each ministry environment should be designed to do no more than one or two things well.

4. *Teach Less for More.* The less you say, the more you will communicate. You will be more effective at every level of your organization if you say only what you need to say to the people who need to hear it.

5. *Listen to Outsiders.* The needs and interests of insiders have a tendency to determine the agenda for the organization. This is especially true of the church. Focus your efforts on those you're trying to reach, rather than on those you're trying to keep.

6. *Replace Yourself.* One day someone else will be doing what you are doing. Whether you have an exit strategy or not, ultimately, you *will* exit. So embrace the inevitable and prepare now for the future.

7. *Work On It.* To maintain your relevance, your sanity, and your effectiveness, you must carve out time in your schedule to step back and evaluate what you are doing and how you are doing it.

Notice something missing? Conspicuously absent here is any discussion about prayer, the Holy Spirit, and dependence upon God. Though absent from the book, these things are certainly not absent from the culture of North Point or from any healthy church.

In fact, the seven practices have proven an answer to our fervent prayers as we sought to create a church that reflects the mission of our Savior. We are convinced that these practices are practical expressions of how the Holy Spirit has chosen to work through the local church. And we have come to depend more on God and less on ourselves as these practices have forced us to let go of some comfortable yet ineffective approaches to ministry.

PLAY BALL!

As you are about to discover, this book is divided into two sections. It begins with a story written by Lane Jones, one of North Point's original six staff members. The narrative focuses on a pastor who plays hooky from an elders' meeting to attend a major league baseball game. That evening, within the context of that single game of baseball, the pastor discovers seven principles that form the basis of the seven practices.

In the second half of the book, another of our original staff members, Reggie Joiner, will delve more deeply into each of the seven practices. He will also share a few pages from North Point's "playbook" to let you see how these practices have been put into action in a ministry setting. Speaking on behalf of our entire team, we can tell you from experience that these principles work.

If you are reading this book alone, I suggest you read it straight through. If you are working through these pages as a team, my recommendation is that you first read a chapter of the parable, then read and discuss the corresponding chapter in the second section. This will give your team an opportunity to evaluate your current ministry environments within the context of each of the seven practices.

Consider this book your ministry's own spring training. As you begin this new season in your ministry and begin to establish each of these seven practices on your team, you will soon find that together you are able to create extraordinary ministry environments—environments that will make your church irresistible to believers and unbelievers alike.

Andy Stanley

Part

I

GETTING IN THE GAME

Ray's Story

1

THE BEST-LAID PLANS

The northbound traffic on the Meadowland Parkway was bumper to bumper. Cars, vans, and SUVs crammed with people of all shapes and sizes moved slowly toward VisionTel Stadium. Children clutching pennants and baseball gloves—and hopes of catching a miraculous foul ball—anxiously waited for their cars to inch ahead. This evening's game was a sellout, and the fans were out in full force. Everyone with a ticket to today's game was pumped.

Everyone except Ray Martin.

Ray was southbound on the parkway. As he passed the stadium on his right, he glanced down at the ticket on the seat next to him. It was a gift from a friend who had connections with the team. A friend he would soon have to call with bad news.

Ray had planned the perfect day: church in the morning, first pitch at 1:00 p.m., and back to church that night for a board meeting. That was before a nine-game winning streak landed his team in first place and ESPN selected this game as their Sunday night game of the week. As a result, the game time had been moved to 8:00. So now, instead of an afternoon of baseball, he was headed for an evening of bedlam at a meeting of the board of the Meadowland Community Church. Ray's eyes narrowed and his forehead creased as he glanced at the northbound lanes of traffic headed to *his* game.

Who could blame him for being upset? No one in their right mind would choose a board meeting over a pitching duel between two potential Cy Young winners. Ray had no reason for feeling guilty. Not even the pastor would blame him for wanting to go to the game.

Unfortunately for Ray, he was the pastor.

Ray had pastored Meadowland for ten years, and until recently, he had never thought of his circumstance as unfortunate. In fact, Ray was the founding pastor—he and he alone was responsible for the church's fate. Or at least it felt that way. Lost in his thoughts, Ray barely heard his cell phone ringing. He grabbed it just before it went to voicemail.

"This is Ray," he said.

"Are you ready for a great game?" the voice on the other end asked. It was Joe Dickinson, the friend who had given him the ticket.

"Oh, hi Joe. I was about to call you. About the game…"

"From the sound of your voice, I'd say you aren't too excited about it," Joe said, interrupting him.

"Let's just say the evening doesn't look too promising."

"Doesn't look promising?" Joe said, "This could be the game of the year!"

"Yeah, well, I wasn't sure how I was going to tell you this, but I can't go to the game, Joe. I have a board meeting at the church, and with the new game time I just can't make it."

"I was afraid of that," Joe said. "Listen, I know it's tough for you to do, but I think you'll be glad you skipped the meeting and went to this game."

I'd skip this meeting for a root canal, Ray thought. "Well, you're probably right, but there's a lot going on right now, and I'd better be there," he said dutifully.

"Well, you do what you have to do," Joe said.

"Thanks for the thought, Joe. I'll try to find someone to use the ticket," Ray offered.

"No, you keep the ticket. I really believe that you *and* the church will be better off if you go to the game, so we'll just see what happens. I'll talk to you later, Ray. Bye."

Ray was puzzled by his friend's comment, and it added to his growing sense of resentment about the board meeting. It wasn't too long ago that the excitement level Ray felt over a baseball game was dwarfed by the excitement of leading Meadowland, but not anymore. In all honesty, it wasn't that he wanted to go to the game as much as he *didn't* want to go to the church.

Ray was headed south in more ways than one.

⚾　⚾　⚾

Ray and his wife Sally, along with twelve others, had begun the church in a nearby home. Their vision was pure and simple: to introduce people into a relationship with Jesus Christ. More than a vision, it was a passion. Ray met Sally while he was in seminary. She was a schoolteacher, and he loved her enthusiasm for changing young lives. She loved his single-mindedness and the passion he had for reaching people for Christ. Together they would change the world, or at least their corner of it. That was before things got so complicated.

It wasn't that Meadowland was a failure as a church. As their area of town exploded, so did their attendance. In ten years the church had grown from a handful of members to over three hundred. They had to be doing *something* right.

If only Ray knew what it was.

It's not that he didn't know what he was doing. Ray was a good speaker, and he knew how to run a church. He just had a nagging sense that lately the church had begun to run *him*.

Their biggest growth had happened in year three when the church opened its new building. Along with the people had come a mortgage and a building committee. Finances, which were always important, became the primary focus of Ray's world. With the building came a ball field and a recreation ministry that "just made sense" and also made some much-needed money.

Year four brought a successful Mother's Day Out Program to generate revenue for the new building and, after all, would "reach the community as well." From there it was a small step to a full preschool and kindergarten program in year five, and *their* success had led to the topic for tonight's board meeting: a new elementary school. In ten short years, Ray had become a pastor, a financier, a recreation director, and now, perhaps, a principal. What he didn't know was *how* or *why* he had become all of those things.

⊘ ⊘ ⊘

The elementary school was the brainchild of Rick Stevens. Rick was a young up-and-comer in the community who had plenty of great ideas about what *other* people should do. This was never more true than at church. It wasn't that his ideas were bad; in fact, they were often quite good. But with them came a sense that Rick had his own agenda. Interestingly enough, he had a set of twins moving into kindergarten.

Rick would be at tonight's meeting.

"Doesn't the school make sense in the grand scheme of things?" Ray had been asked. "Why let all those Sunday school rooms sit empty during the week? Won't the kindergarten graduates need a good school to go to? Won't it bring in more people from the community?"

But who's going to hire all of those teachers? he thought. *And who's going to select the curriculum? Who's going to schedule the fire drills and run the PTA?* Ray knew whom the *who* was, and it wasn't Rick. The *who* was *him*, and Ray could feel it in the pit of his stomach.

The traffic to the game stretched out across from him as a nagging reminder that his day had been ruined. A day of relaxing fun had become a Maalox moment.

Why shouldn't I get to go to the game? he thought. *Is it my fault they moved the time? Is it my fault Rick had to have a school? I've missed board meetings before. There was that time I was on a mission trip, and the time Sally was in labor. We always survived. Besides, this is going to be a great game. Don't I deserve a life? Where is it written that the pastor can't enjoy himself a little now and then?*

Ray's stomach lurched as he thought about adding another large leadership helping to his already full plate. How could he keep all those balls in the air? Sally and the kids would suffer. His preaching would surely suffer. The rest of the church would probably suffer, too.

If only he didn't have to go to this meeting.

If only Rick didn't have children.

If only Ray could turn the car around and head for the game.

There was his chance, a cut in the median that offered him the opportunity of escape. All it would take is a turn of the steering wheel and he'd be free. One turn and anguish would become ecstasy.

One turn and, suddenly, Ray was northbound on the Meadowland Parkway.

⚾   ⚾   ⚾

It took him a moment to realize what he had done. The car horn behind him blasted him back to reality. His was now one of hundreds of automobiles headed for the ballpark.

You can't do this! Ray's conscience screamed. *You're the pastor, for God's sake. And I do mean for God's sake. He wants you there. Who's going to lead the meeting?*

Actually, Ray knew that with or without him, Jim Benson would be leading the meeting. Jim was the chairman of the elder board and a good man. Ray had had the wisdom to not only share the burden of leadership with an elder board, but to protect himself by not being its chairman. Ray wasn't looking forward to that phone call: "Hi Jim, it's Ray. By the way, I know you're a volunteer and I'm paid to be there, but I won't be at the meeting tonight, okay? Great. Gotta go." There was no way to make it sound good.

Maybe I could tell him I'm sick, Ray thought. *Sure, why not compound my lack of leadership with a lack of integrity, too?*

No, the only thing to do was to call Jim and tell him the truth. Tell him that when his pastor faced the toughest leadership decision of his career, he boldly stepped forward and went to a ball game.

"What a loser," Ray said out loud without thinking.

The ring of the cell phone sounded like an alarm announcing a prison break. Ray looked at the caller ID. Jim Benson.

Great. I've been caught. Barely over the wall, and I'm going back in, he thought.

"Hi, this is Ray," he answered.

"Ray, Jim Benson."

"Hi Jim, how are you?"

"I'm fine," Jim said. "Listen, I know this is last-minute, but I've talked to almost all of the guys on the board, and it looks like we're going to be a little short on attendance tonight."

"Really, Jim? How short?" A small ray of hope flickered.

"Well, Rick Stevens will be there, even though he's not on the board. But with him, it looks like there will be two."

Two? Ray's mind raced. How could Jim already know that he wasn't coming?

"I'm sorry, Ray," Jim finally said. "I know it was a big meeting, but something has come up and I can't be there either. I hate it, I really do."

"You mean *none* of the elders can be there?" Ray asked, trying to disguise his great relief. "I don't believe it."

"I know it, Ray. I'm embarrassed to even call myself the chairman. I'd understand if you wanted me to resign."

"What? Oh no, I don't want you to give it another thought," Ray said. *I know I won't.* "We'll just regroup for next month's meeting and cover everything then. Could you do me a little favor, Jim?"

"You name it."

"Could you call Rick and tell him that we're postponing the meeting?" Ray knew that he should make the call, but he couldn't pass up the chance to leverage Jim's guilt.

"No problem. I'll call him as soon as we're done," Jim said graciously. So graciously that now it was Ray who felt guilty. "Thanks again for understanding, Ray. I'll talk to you later."

"What kind of pastor would I be if I weren't understanding?" Ray said, surprisingly without choking. "I'll talk to you soon."

It took a couple of minutes for the full impact of the conversation to hit Ray. Not only was he getting to go to a great ball game, he was avoiding the embarrassing situation of showing up at a difficult meeting without answers.

I still need the answers, he thought, *but I'll think about that later. God has granted me a reprieve, and I intend on taking the night off.*

Ray had rarely been more wrong.

2

THROWING STRIKES

It was almost game time when Ray arrived at the ballpark. Traffic was still bad and hopes for seeing the first pitch were fading. He tried Joe's cell phone but only got his voicemail.

I hope he doesn't decide not to show. Just my luck...

Ray decided not to finish the thought, considering the recent turn of events. At this point the game could be rained out and Ray would still consider himself a lucky man.

It was strange, though, that the entire board would suddenly be busy. No more strange, Ray decided, than a grown man making a last-second U-turn to avoid a meeting that *he* had called.

I must be more confused than I thought, Ray admitted to himself.

Unaccustomed to the new ballpark, Ray gave the attendant the parking pass that came with his ticket.

"This is for the Gold lot, sir. Turn right here and through that gate. You have a great time."

Ray turned into the gate and suddenly the traffic disappeared. He was on an open driveway, and in two minutes he was literally in the shadow of the stadium. Seeing the start of the game was looking more promising. Another parking attendant signaled for Ray to stop and approached the car. *This is where I get sent to the Siberia lot,* Ray thought.

"Good evening, sir," the young man said. "Welcome to VisionTel Stadium. I'll be glad to park your car. Please hold onto this ticket, and we'll return the car to this spot after the game."

Joe must have better connections than I thought. Glancing at the toys and the occasional wayward french fry scattered on the floorboard, Ray self-consciously turned the keys over to the young man.

"I bet you're not used to a ride like this one."

"No, sir." The young man smiled.

"What's the best way to get to my seat?" Ray showed him the ticket.

"Straight through that door. Just show the lady the ticket, and she'll direct you."

Ray made his way toward the door with a sign above it that read, "Restricted Access."

This must be a mistake, he thought.

"Good evening, sir. May I see your ticket?"

Ray handed his ticket to the lady at the door. "I may be in the wrong place," he explained.

"Oh no, sir. Please follow me." She led Ray down a long corridor. "Not too much further," she said as they approached another door. "Here we are."

She opened the door, and the sounds of the ballpark came flooding in. The persistent buzz of the crowd and the organ music on the PA system mingled with the nostalgic smell of popcorn, peanuts, and beer.

Ray found himself in the field level section.

"May I see your ticket, sir?" a female attendant asked. Ray obliged. "This way, sir." Ray followed as the attendant led him down the aisle past row after row. The startlingly green grass was close enough to smell, and the voices of the players could be heard as they called out to one another. Ray was finally ushered to one of only two seats left on this side of the railing. One more step and he would be on the field.

"Can I get you anything else, sir?"

"Is there more?" Ray responded without thinking. The attendant smiled as if she was accustomed to delivering mere mortals into baseball heaven.

"Enjoy the game," she said. "If you want anything, a server will take your order."

A server will take my order, he thought. *And to think I almost missed this to go to a board meeting.* The thought of the meeting reminded Ray that there was a harsh reality out there waiting for him after the game. A reality that right now was filled with more questions than answers.

Why can't real life be like a ball game? he thought.

⚾ ⚾ ⚾

"Excuse me. Excuse me, but I can't get to my seat." The voice startled Ray from his thoughts. He had been so awed by his surroundings and newfound status that he hadn't heard the gentleman the first time.

"I'm sorry," Ray said.

"Oh, no problem. It's an amazing place, isn't it?" the older man said as he sat down and looked around the park.

Ray realized that there were no more open seats nearby, and the one he had assumed was for Joe was now taken. "Are you sure you have the right section?" Ray asked the question as if he was a regular.

"Oh yes, I'm pretty sure," the man replied. "Row one, seat one. And you *are* Ray, aren't you?"

Now the sublime had become surreal. Customer service was one thing, but now Ray was entering the Twilight Zone. "Have we met?" he asked the older man.

"My name is Pete. I'm a friend of Joe's. He told me you'd be here."

"So Joe won't be here tonight?"

"Well, you never know with Joe. He didn't tell you about me, did he?"

"Obviously not." Ray didn't try to hide his confusion or his disappointment.

"Well, I hope you still enjoy the game," Pete said. "It should be a good one. What do you do for a living, Ray?"

Now Ray was a little embarrassed by his response to Pete. "I'm, uh, a pastor. At a church near here."

"A pastor, huh? I think Joe did mention that. Although he's never sent me a pastor before. This could be interesting. Of course, it could be a waste of time, too."

"I'm sorry, but am I supposed to know what you're talking about?"

"No. Would you like a hot dog or a beer? Oh, of course you don't want a beer," Pete said laughing. "How about a soft drink?"

"If this night gets any stranger, I may take you up on that beer. But for now a bottle of water would be great."

Pete glanced over his shoulder and instantly an attendant was there to take the order. Ray was impressed by the immediate attention that this unimpressive man received. Not that there was anything wrong with Pete. There was just nothing *special* about him. He looked to be in his mid-sixties. Slightly overweight and balding, with gray hair. His eyes were very clear, though, like the eyes of a much younger man.

"Just what is it that you do, Pete?" he finally asked.

"Oh, a little of this, a little of that."

Ray couldn't help but think that his job description pretty much summed up his appearance. The attendant quickly returned with their order. "Here you are, Mr. Harlan. Can I get you anything else?"

"Not right now, Jenny, but thanks."

Pete Harlan? Ray thought. *I know I've heard that name before, but where?*

A young man came out of the dugout and handed Pete a pair of binoculars.

Then it hit him. "You're Peter J. Harlan." Ray said more than asked. "You own the team."

"So I've heard," Pete replied. "Around here, though, I'm just a fan like anyone else. Except I get the best seats, don't you think?"

Suddenly it all made sense. The valet parking, the great seats, the quick service. No wonder Joe kept insisting that he come to the game. But why? Joe was a good friend, but there had to be more to it than that.

"Mr. Harlan, can I ask—"

"Pete. Call me Pete."

"Very well, Pete. You said earlier that he had never sent you a pastor before. What did you mean?"

"You caught that, did you? Sometimes my mouth pops the clutch before my mind gets in gear. You see, Ray, I have a passion for creating winning organizations. I've done it in business for years. In fact, that's why I bought this baseball team. I love to see a group of people working together toward a common vision, and I've had some success in doing it."

"That's an understatement," Ray said. Harlan Enterprises was one of the most successful corporations in the area. Real estate, manufacturing, data processing and storage were just a few of the markets he had dominated. "I know your track record, Mr. Harlan…"

Pete held up a hand to stop him. "It's Pete, remember?"

"I know your track record, Pete, but what does that have to do with my being here?"

"Well, from time to time Joe brings me a young leader who he feels could gain something from my experience. I like to meet with them and find out what's going on and then see if I can help. Joe obviously thinks I have something to offer you."

How about a big contribution to the building fund? he wanted to say. It made him nervous to sit so close to a man who could end all of his financial troubles with one check.

Ray decided to ignore the fact that Joe thought he could use some help, but he couldn't so quickly dismiss the doubt that this business-man could help a pastor. "So I'm the first pastor Joe's ever brought you?" he finally said. "Well, at least we'll see a good game."

"You seem unsure about the value of our time together, Ray."

Ray's expression had given away more than he thought. "It's not that I'm uncertain, it's just that I don't know if you have a clear under-standing of what it takes to run a church."

"Well, as long as you're not uncertain," Pete replied with a hint of sarcasm. He had seen this before. The first step was always the most difficult: getting a young leader to recognize that before cir-cumstances could change, *he* might have to change. "It seems to me that church work is a lot like any other business. You have a prod-uct, you have customers, and you have salesmen. The only difference is that you have God on your side and that should make it easier, right?"

"You'd think so, wouldn't you?" Ray said. His vision of a relaxing night off was beginning to fade. The last thing he wanted to think about was his inability to run his church, even with God's help. But before he could say anything, Pete broke the silence.

"Why don't you tell me a little about your church, Ray?"

So Ray gave Pete the brochure-copy tour of Meadowland Community Church. He talked about the years of growth, the variety of ministries, and the growing facility. The family atmosphere among the congregation sounded almost too good to be true. And some of it was. Obviously, Joe thought there was room for improvement, but Ray could figure it out without Pete's help. After all, why should he share his struggles with a man he barely knew and who obviously knew no struggles.

"It sounds like a great place, Ray. I can't imagine why Joe wanted us to meet," Pete said.

"I was wondering the same thing." Ray tried not to sound too defensive.

"Well, why don't we just hang out together and watch the game. If it's okay with you, I might offer a few insights as the night goes on."

"It's your ball game," Ray said, not fully appreciating the irony of the statement.

"It is, isn't it?" Pete said. "Ray, I need you to do me a favor."

"What's that?"

"In a moment, a man is going to walk over here with a baseball. I need you to take it out to the mound and throw it to the catcher."

"You want *what*?" Ray sputtered. "You...you want me to throw out the first pitch?"

"Call it an owner's privilege, but yeah, I want you to throw out the first pitch. But one more thing, Ray: I want you to throw a strike."

Before Ray had time to think about it, a man wearing a team jacket came over and handed him a hat and a brand-new baseball. It had been years since Ray had held one, having graduated on to the safer, more age-appropriate softball. He felt the seams between his fingers as he began to consider which pitch he would throw. A two-seam fastball seemed the obvious choice since it was the only pitch Ray knew how to throw. In a daze, he made his way to the mound, as his name and image appeared on the Jumbotron. The stadium grew a little louder as the crowd anticipated the start of the game and the possibility that this unknown man in slacks and a buttoned-down dress shirt would bounce a pitch to the backstop.

This game is on ESPN! Ray's mind screamed as he stood on the mound. *One screwup and I'll land in the SportsCenter Hall of Shame.* As if in slow motion, the catcher squatted behind the plate and motioned to Ray to let her fly. Without thinking and without stretching, Ray drew his arm back and did his best John Smoltz impersonation. He watched as the ball fluttered with an un-Smoltz-like velocity toward the plate and fell neatly, if not powerfully, into the catcher's mitt. The crowd cheered, as much in relief that the game could start, as it was a favorable response to Ray's handiwork.

Ray, on the other hand, was pumped. He bounced off the mound and removed his cap in a grand gesture of appreciation. He shook the catcher's hand and, after an obligatory photo that Ray would hang on his office wall forever, he headed toward his seat.

"Not bad," Pete said as Ray arrived. "I wasn't certain you had a clear understanding of what it takes to throw a baseball."

Ray got the point immediately and decided to accept the mild criticism without comment. After all, he was a guest and he had just thrown a strike in "The Show."

3

KEEPING SCORE

"Ray, what was your goal when you headed out onto that field just now?" Pete asked.

"Well, beyond not falling down and making a fool out of myself, I guess it was to throw a strike."

"Why?"

"Because you asked me to?"

"And you did it, didn't you?"

"Yeah, I guess I did."

"How does it feel?"

"Pretty good, I guess." Ray wasn't sure where this was headed, but he hoped that Pete wasn't one of those "positive thinkers" who talked about visualizing world peace. Right about now, Ray was visualizing a quick dash for the parking lot if the conversation got too strange.

"It's a funny thing, Ray. People like to win."

Ray looked around for the fortune cookie that had given Pete *that* gem.

"Ray, when is the last time you left a church service or a meeting feeling the way you did when you left that mound just now? When's the last time you *won* at church?"

Ray was stunned. He wanted to tell this pompous, not-a-care-in-the-world billionaire just what he thought; the problem was, Ray didn't *know* what he thought. He only knew it had been years since he had felt that kind of excitement about his ministry.

"It's okay, Ray. The truth is, I set you up. I know it's a lousy trick, but it works every time. The problem is that right now you're thinking you're not a winner, but that's really not your problem."

Confused but curious, Ray asked, "Then what is my problem?"

"When you went out to that mound, it was to throw a strike, right?"

"Right."

"You knew that to win, you had to throw a strike. Your problem is, you don't know what a *win* is at church, do you?"

"Well," Ray began slowly, "it's a lot of things. It's a good service on Sunday morning and a good children's program. It's missions and music and a lot of things that are a little more complicated than throwing a baseball."

Pete could see Ray's frustration growing. "You're right, a win at church is more complicated; so knowing what a win looks like is all the more important. What do you see out there in right field, just above the Home Depot sign?"

"The scoreboard."

"Right. Nothing but zeros up there right now, but what's going to happen every time one of our players crosses home plate?"

"We'll score a run."

"Right. And a run will go on the board, and we'll be ahead, and all of these people will cheer."

"But we don't have a scoreboard in the sanctuary, and the only plate we have is an offering plate. And I can assure you that no one cheers when we pass it."

Pete laughed. "That much I remember about church. The point is, Ray, you need to know when you're getting ahead, and your people need to know when to cheer. That's the first step: *Clarify the Win*. There's not a player on that field right now who's confused about his goal. They may not reach it, but they know what it is. If you give good people a clear goal, then most of the time they'll work like dogs to get there. But if the goal is unclear, they're forced to guess or, worse, decide for themselves what a win really is.

**Practice #1
Clarify the Win**

"The truth of the matter is that with or without a goal, they're going to work hard to get *somewhere*. That's the thing about leaders—they lead. The question is, Are they getting where you want them to go?"

Ray thought of Rick Stevens. Rick was a leader, and he was leading Ray right into an unwanted job as school principal. Ray had never thought of this as being his own fault, though. It was easier to blame Rick and to focus on his ulterior motives. It could be that Rick Stevens was just leading in a direction that no one had told him not to.

Ray had to admit that it was difficult to tell when things were working well at the church. Multiple programs meant multiple problems and much-needed solutions. Further difficulties were created when a solution in one area caused more problems in another.

"So how do you do it?" he asked. "How do you clarify the win?"

"Just ask yourself, *What is the most important thing?* and it will start to become clear. For our team, it's winning ball games. Sure, I'm here to make money, but the easiest way to make money in baseball is by winning. So what is it for you, Ray? What's most important?"

Pete thought this might be a good time for a deep breath and a hot dog. He motioned for the attendant and with a simple nod of his head ordered his guest and himself "the usual." The two men sat and watched as the home team took the field and the game began.

"Changed lives," Ray finally said.

"What's that, Ray?"

"You asked what a win is. It's a life that's been changed—that's a win."

"Well, there you go. Ray, from what you've told me, things are going pretty well at your church. If you'd like, we can just sit back and enjoy the game."

Ray wasn't sure what had just happened, but he knew that he wouldn't be enjoying the game. *Of course* life change was the goal; he had been called to make disciples. This was not news to Ray. His original doubts about the value of this conversation were beginning to rise again. "You said clarifying the win was the first step. Just how many steps are there?"

"Seven." Pete said matter-of-factly, watching the action on the field. "But they're not all steps. Think of them as *practices*."

"Seven practices?" Ray asked.

"Seven practices for effective business—or in your case, I guess, effective ministry. I've watched these seven practices work in a variety of situations, and apparently Joe thinks they can help you, too. But like I said, it's no big deal to me if you just want to watch the game and enjoy the evening."

This was music to Ray's ears. A nice relaxing evening was all he really wanted. So Ray was surprised to hear himself saying, "If the first practice is *clarify the win*, what's the second one?"

4

GETTING ON BASE

Pete had learned to recognize that look of hungry desperation in the eyes of a young leader. The look that says, *I may not know what I'm doing, but I care enough to find out why.*

"Well, once you've clarified the win, you have to figure out the best way to get there. And for you, this is where it gets really practical. You can remain philosophical about life change being the win and lives won't change. Or you can figure out where and how life change happens best and then move people there."

"What do you mean?" Ray asked.

"Like I said before, the goal in baseball is to get to home plate. That's where a win occurs. *You* have to decide where a win happens best for you. Is it your Sunday morning service or somewhere else? Once you know where it is, then you have to take the steps necessary to get there."

"Pete?" Ray interrupted, "I hate to interrupt again, but I was planning on watching a baseball game tonight, not taking notes."

"Look, son, I said we could just watch the game, but you asked me what the second…"

"No, it's not that," Ray stammered. "I was just wondering if you had anything I could write some of this down on?"

Pete smiled. "Sure, Ray. No problem." Pete motioned for the attendant, and in no time Ray had a pad and clipboard bearing the team logo.

"As I was saying," Pete continued, "in baseball, the first step is getting to first base. It's the first step for any batter. The ultimate goal is to get home and score, but you can't do that without getting to first. You see this guy coming to the plate right now?" he asked.

Ray recognized the opposing player. "Yes."

"He's one of their best hitters and fastest runners. That's why he's at the top of their lineup. His goal is to get on first. Then he must find a way, with the help of his team, to get to second, third, and finally home."

Thanks for clearing that up, Ray thought.

"This isn't rocket science, Ray. All I'm saying is that you have to figure out the best way to change lives and do that one step at a time. In other words, *Think Steps, Not Programs.*"

"But there are a lot of ways to effect life change," Ray said defensively. He was thinking about the weekly calendar of events at the church: Sunday morning services, Sunday school, Sunday night service, Monday night visitation, Wednesday night prayer meeting, leadership meetings, recreation leagues, and now the prospect of a school on top of all of that. "Programs lead to life change," he finally said.

"They can lead to life change or they can just become a way of life," Pete offered. "The tendency in business, or in church work for that matter, is to mistake activity for progress. We think that just because people are busy and doing a lot of stuff that we are being successful. The fact of the matter is, if all that activity isn't taking you where you want to go, then it's just wasted time. You see, Ray, it's not enough that you clarify the win if how to get there is unclear or, worse, impossible. In fact, you'll frustrate people more by giving them a clear vision without a strategy for achieving it."

Practice #2
Think Steps, Not Programs

"So what makes a good step?"

"It has to be *easy*, *obvious*, and *strategic*," Pete said.

Ray held his hand up to stop Pete as he wrote furiously on his pad. "What do those terms mean?"

"If it's not *easy* for people to do, then they won't do it. You can blame their lack of commitment if you want, but ultimately it's *your* fault because you expected too much out of them. I learned that early on with some of my Internet dealings. One of my companies tried to pump up their Internet sales but the effort fell flat. It turns out that people *wanted* to buy online but our process was so difficult that the majority of buyers quit in the middle of the transaction. It wasn't *easy*."

"But sometimes things that are valuable don't come that easily," Ray countered.

"That's why you break them down into steps that are easy. That way you raise the likelihood of achieving your goal. Second, a good step has to be *obvious*, or your people may go the wrong way. This is sort of like clarifying the win on each step. You don't want them to have to guess where second base is. And finally, and most importantly, it has to be *strategic*."

"Strategic?"

"In other words, it's part of a strategy for moving your people from one place to another, from first to second to third and then home. In your case, from one place in their lives to another. If a program isn't a step that is part of a strategy, then it can waste a lot of time and money and, in your case, life."

"I don't think we've started any bad programs yet," Ray said, trying not to be defensive.

"That's the problem, Ray. It's usually good things that knock you off target."

Now Ray was getting a headache.

"Ray, do you remember Johnny Tuminello?"

"The all-star third baseman? Sure. I still can't believe you let him get away."

"Get away? I traded him on purpose."

"Why? He was great! Forty-two home runs and runner-up for the batting title, if I remember correctly."

"Oh, you remember correctly. What you don't know is that he was more concerned with his personal stats and marketability than he was with the success of the team. He was a great player, but he wasn't great for the team. In the same way, you can cover your people up with programs that look great on the outside, but without a strategy you won't end up where you want. It's like the old adage that a flood is just a river that couldn't decide where it wanted to go."

Ray had to admit that he had never thought of ministry in those terms. He had done what he had *always seen* done in much the same way it had *always been* done. What would a strategy for changing lives look like? What steps were missing? Which ones had he stumbled onto without even knowing?

5

STAYING FOCUSED

"Okay. First, clarify the win. Then think steps, not programs. Now what?"

"Wouldn't you rather watch the game, Ray?"

"I would have loved to, but since you've already ruined my evening, I might as well get the whole treatment," Ray said, laughing.

"All right, you asked for it. Practice number three is this: *Narrow the Focus*. By that I mean you shouldn't try to do everything; you should do a *few* things *well*."

"Right. Think steps, not programs. We've already covered that," Ray said.

"You learn quickly. There are similarities, but *narrow the focus* is…well, it's more focused. While it does apply to the *number* of things you do, it also applies to the *way* you do the things you do. Once you've created a step that's easy, obvious, and strategic, you need to make sure that that step stays focused. Don't try to make it do something that it wasn't created to do. Do you see that guy out there?" Pete asked pointing to the mound.

"The pitcher?" Ray asked. "Yeah, he's one of my favorites."

"Do you know how much I pay him every year?"

"No."

"Well, in your terms, I'm guessing it would be two sanctuaries and about twenty thousand square feet of nursery space."

"That much, huh?"

"Yep. Do you know what his batting average was last year?"

"No."

".094.... I paid a man over fourteen million dollars who got a hit *less than ten percent of the time.* I don't think he had one RBI all season. But he can throw a baseball ninety-eight miles an hour over either corner of the plate. Do you get my point?"

"I have a feeling I'm about to."

"Pitchers don't need to *hit* well; they need to *pitch* well. Every step you create needs to do what it does best and nothing more. Focus allows you to pursue excellence, to zero in on the target. You can ruin a great pitcher by trying to make a hitter out of him, and you can ruin a great church..."

"...by making a school out of it," Ray said without thinking.

"Where did that come from?" Pete asked.

"Oh, just something I've been thinking a lot about lately."

"Joe said you were facing some tough calls, but he didn't tell me what they were," Pete said.

Ray had forgotten about Joe's involvement in all of this. Is this why he arranged the tickets to the game, to forestall the school decision? *No,* Ray thought, *he couldn't have known for sure that I would be able to make it tonight. Anyway, it was the AWOL elder board that canceled the meeting.*

"Ray, are you with me?"

"Oh, sorry. I guess I'm a little distracted. So you don't think a church should start a school?"

"I didn't say that. What I said was, you can ruin one thing by trying to get it to do something else. Babe Ruth entered the big leagues as a pitcher, and he was a *good* pitcher. What do you think would've happened if he had focused on his pitching?"

"Good pitcher, but no home run record?"

"Probably. Now it's possible that the Babe could've won three hundred games and hit seven hundred home runs, but not very likely. The question is, Do you want to have a great church or a great school? Because the chances of having both are about the same as the Babe's."

Practice #3
Narrow the Focus

Ray thought about this for a minute. He had always assumed they could have a great church *and* a great school. But what Pete was saying made sense. They had to make a choice. Every minute he spent on the school would be one he couldn't spend on the church.

"Narrowing the focus *seems* so limiting," Ray finally said, "but when you think about it, it really frees you up to do *more*. You just do one thing really well."

"Now you're getting it."

"It's more than narrowing the focus though," Ray said. "For me, it's personally clarifying the win. God called me to start a church, not a school. My win is the church."

"That's great, Ray. When these practices work together, when you don't have competing visions or cross-purposes, there's a refreshing simplicity and efficiency to your organization. Practice number four is really an extension of that idea."

6

TEACHING THE FUNDAMENTALS

"I don't have to tell you that I don't know a whole lot about running a church," Pete said. "But as I thought about meeting with you tonight, this next practice was the one that I wished more preachers would try. I call it, *Teach Less for More*."

"Teach less for more?" Ray asked. "Are you saying we need shorter sermons?"

"Well, it probably wouldn't hurt. But no, that's not what it means. In my business career I've found that most people confuse the quantity of information communicated with the quality of implementation in the workplace. They think that the more I tell them, the better they'll do. But I have learned a very important business lesson watching my baseball team."

"What's that?" Ray asked, as he realized for the first time that he really wanted to know.

"Baseball players really only need to know a few things to do their jobs. They need to know how to throw a ball, catch a ball, hit a ball, and run like mad. No matter what we tell them, if it doesn't help in one of those categories, then it really doesn't help. For instance, do you see the guy playing second base?"

"Raphael Ortega?"

"Yeah, that's right. He doesn't speak a word of English. But he can turn a double play like no one else in the league, and he's a great lead-off hitter. My staff could knock themselves out teaching him English so he could learn the managerial strategy of baseball, not to mention the business strategy for running the team, but it wouldn't make him a better second baseman."

"That's *narrow the focus* again."

"Very good. I told you they were connected, but it is a little different. *Narrow the focus* says to do one thing and do it well. *Teach less for more* applies that practice to the information you communicate to your people. That's why it jumped out at me when I thought about meeting with you. I went to church my entire childhood, and do you know what I learned?"

"What?"

"Not a thing. I know I heard a lot of things about God, but I don't remember one of them."

"Maybe you didn't have good teachers."

"How good do you have to be to teach a child one thing? No, the problem wasn't that they couldn't teach me one thing. The problem was they tried to teach me *everything*. Every week was a different story and a different lesson with a different picture. All I knew is that if I sat there quietly, I'd get a cookie at the end."

"So you did learn something," Ray said with a smile. "I get your point. We do tend to think more is better when sometimes it's just more." Ray thought about this for a minute. "What if we boiled it down to just the basics? You know, hitting and catching. Or in our case loving God, loving others, and loving yourself."

"But don't forget to narrow the focus," Pete said. "We have to focus on baseball players. *You* have to take those basics and focus on children, teenagers, and adults. They don't all need to know the same things."

"Are you sure you've never run a church before?" Ray asked.

"I've run *from* church before, does that count?" Pete laughed. "It's all about getting the right information to the right people in the right position. That's why we have coaches on the field during the game. A player who's batting or running the bases can't be expected to keep up with the overall strategy of the game. So we have a first-base coach and a third-base coach continually feeding them the information they need to be successful. Not to mention another group of coaches and a manager putting players in the right positions. As the leader of your organization, that's your job, too."

Practice #4
Teach Less for More

The ball game had continued, although Ray had hardly noticed. The excitement of the game, the field-level seats, and the VIP treatment had begun to be replaced by an excitement that Ray hadn't felt in a while. His hand ached as he scribbled down Pete's insights as well as his own ideas of how to implement them. The problems that had haunted him earlier began to look more like challenges. Did this mean that he had to start over from scratch? Would everyone at the church think he'd lost his mind when he started talking about clarifying wins and teaching less for more?

"Pete, can we recap for just a second? I want to make sure I'm understanding all of this."

"Sure, why don't you read back to me what you have, and I'll fill in any gaps."

"All right," Ray said as he looked over his notes. "Practice one is *clarify the win*."

"And the point?" Pete asked.

"If you give people a clear target, then they're more likely to hit it."

"Good. And number two?"

"*Think steps, not programs*. Because you shouldn't start anything that doesn't get you where you want to go."

"Number three?" Pete asked.

"*Narrow the focus*."

"Why?"

"Because if you try to do everything you'll end up with nothing."

"Excellent!" Even Pete was getting excited now. "And number four?"

"*Teach less for more* because everyone doesn't need to know everything. It's more important to get the right information to the right people."

"You're a quick study, Ray. So is all of this overwhelming or helpful?" Pete asked.

"Can it be both?"

"Yeah." Pete laughed. "It may help to think of the first four practices as a way of keeping your organization in alignment."

"Alignment?"

"Have you ever driven a car that was out of alignment, Ray?"

"Sure."

"What did it do?"

"Well, it pulled to one side and was hard to drive."

"Exactly. In the same way, a church or a business needs to stay in alignment or it can be pulled off course and become difficult to lead. But if you clarify the win, establish clear and focused steps to achieving that win, and communicate the right information to the right people, then chances are you'll stay aligned and headed in the right direction."

"It's funny," Ray finally said, "I've either picked the right people instinctively or been really lucky with certain leaders. I have this great man who chairs the elder board..."

"Jim?"

"Yeah. Jim. He's a great leader for that role. He's steady and balanced and...and how did you know my chairman's name was Jim?"

For the first time, Pete was the speechless one. The awkward look on his face was enough to tell Ray that something was up. "What's going on, Pete?" Ray asked.

"All right, you might as well know. Do you see that skybox up by the Coca-Cola sign?"

"Yeah."

"Take a look with my binoculars." Puzzled, Ray lifted the binoculars and, after a moment, found the box. Seated there, in air-conditioned comfort, were Joe Dickinson, Jim Benson, and the entire elder board of the Meadowland Community Church.

"It's easy to see how conspiracy theories get started, isn't it?" Pete laughed. "Don't take it personally. Most of the guys have no idea you're down here with me. They're up there feeling guilty about missing your meeting."

"Oh yeah," Ray said as he watched through the binoculars, "the guilt is plastered all over their smiling, mustard-stained faces." Ray was about to make a comment about lack of commitment until he remembered the relief he had felt when Jim called to cancel the meeting. In reality, Ray wasn't sure what to think. He didn't know the motivation of his board. Were they relieved to miss the meeting or just happy to go to a great ball game? All he knew was that he was happy to avoid the meeting and that his time with Pete had been very helpful. He knew he had to let Pete off the hook, but it was nice to see this powerful man a little on the defensive. "To be honest with you, Pete, no one was happier to postpone that meeting than I."

"Why, Ray? Why did you dread that meeting so much?"

Ray knew the answer, but actually saying it was harder than he thought. "Because I knew that I didn't have the answers to the questions that were going to be asked. I guess Joe and Jim knew it, too."

"What about now? Are things any clearer or would you rather stop and enjoy the game?" Pete asked sincerely.

As much as he hated to admit it, Ray was wrong about Pete. How could a man who had never been to his church, and rarely to any church as far as Ray knew, understand so much about running one?

"Well," Ray began, "why don't we go ahead and finish?"

"That's why I'm here. But I warn you, the last three may be the toughest."

"Now you're just trying to scare me." Ray laughed.

7

THE ROAR OF
THE CROWD

"The first four practices are all about making changes to the organization." Pete began. "The last three require a personal change for the leader, and sometimes, that's a little more difficult."

"What is practice number five?" Ray asked, ready to write.

"Number five is *Listen to Outsiders*."

"Listening?" Ray responded. "I don't mean to be arrogant here, Pete, but listening is actually something we do pretty well. In fact, I spend most of my time listening."

"Yes. But you listen to problems and provide solutions. I'm talking about listening to people outside of the church for answers, not questions."

Ray thought about this quietly. He wasn't ready to surrender the high ground on this point yet.

Pete broke the silence. "Ray, let me ask you something, and be honest with me and yourself. When you first realized that a tired old businessman who hadn't darkened the door of a church in fifty years was going to give you pointers on running your church, what was your first reaction?"

Ray surrendered the high ground. Embarrassed, he admitted his first reaction to Pete. "'What can this guy possibly tell me about running a church?'"

"You wouldn't be normal if you didn't think that. Most people who run any organization think they know what's best for it, and a lot of the time they do. But if you aren't willing to listen to outsiders, you may miss a great idea or the opportunity to gain market share. And from what I can tell, market share is a big deal in your line of work."

"So how do I get the input of outsiders?" Ray asked.

"You ask questions and then you listen. Fifty years ago baseball was played during the daytime. Some in the game realized that if interest in the game was going to go up, and profits along with it, then we had to gain more fans. Along came television and an opportunity to reach a lot of new fans. But people watch TV at night, so night baseball was the answer. Later, a lot of people would come to a game or two but felt the game itself was too slow or boring. That led to mascots in chicken suits and video arcades, along with Jumbotron screens and batting cages. The point is, we listened to what outsiders were telling us, and we adjusted. If it were up to the insiders, the purists, we'd still be playing day games."

"So whose idea was the strike?" Ray asked.

"What's that?"

"The strike a few years ago. Which outsiders were you guys listening to when you came up with *that* idea?" Ray knew he was treading on thin ice, but he also knew that his profession wasn't the only one that could become insider-focused.

"Well, that was before I got into the game, but you're right. We weren't listening to the fans, and it cost us some of them."

Ray decided to ease the tension. "You don't have to tell me about insiders. Churches are full of them," he said, thinking back on some of the many calls he had received over the years whenever he tried anything new. "The funny thing is, most of them start out as outsiders."

"And that leads to one of the primary reasons that you have to listen to outsiders: If you don't, you will be driven by the complaints and demands of the insiders. And ultimately your market share will dwindle. And in your line of work, there's more at stake than business."

"Pete, if I didn't know better, I'd say you were on our side."

Practice #5
Listen to Outsiders

"The question you have to answer is, What can you learn from the people you're trying to reach? If you watch them and listen to them, they'll tell you what they think and want. Then you just have to figure out how to use that information. Don't be so concerned about keeping the folks you've got, that you neglect the folks you're trying to reach."

"Why do you think this one is harder than the first four practices?"

"Because you have to admit that you don't have all of the answers. And that leads to the frightening realization that there might be someone else out there who can do your job better then you. Which is a scary place to be, unless of course you get there on purpose."

"On purpose?"

"That's right. Practice number six will get you there on purpose."

"In that case, let's stop at number five." Ray said, not sure if he was kidding or not.

8

DEVELOPING NEW TALENT

"We can stop at number five and your organization will last a good, long time. Or we can go on to number six and your organization can last forever." Pete's demeanor said this was less an opinion and more a fact.

Ray knew he had to find out what practice number six was; he just didn't know if he'd like it when he did. Warily, he asked, "Okay then, what's number six?"

Pete's tone became a little more serious. "If you want your church to stand the test of time, then you have to be replaced."

The words hit Ray like a hundred-mile-an-hour fastball. So this was the point of the evening! This was why Jim and Joe and the entire elder board were so willing to miss the meeting and come to the ballpark. Ray could feel the emotion rising up inside of him. Why go through this charade when the bottom line was that he was out as pastor? Why the seven practices? Why the royal treatment? Why not just a quick meeting and then show him the door? Speaking of the door, Ray began to look again for the quickest way out of the stadium.

"Ray? Ray, are you still with me?" Pete asked.

"Not for much longer, apparently," Ray shot back.

"What are you talking about?"

"I'm talking about being replaced. But honestly, I would think that Jim and the board would have the decency to do it themselves and not have a total stranger tell me." The funny thing was, Ray didn't really think of Pete as a total stranger. He had only known this man for a little more than two hours, and yet he thought of him as a friend.

"Wait a minute! Slow down a little. No one is replacing you."

"You just said I was being replaced."

"No, I didn't. I said that if you wanted your church to stand the test of time, you had to be replaced."

From the look on Ray's face, Pete could tell that he had yet to make his point. "Ray, how old are you?"

"Thirty-six going on seventy-seven, right now."

"And how long do you plan on living?"

"What difference does it make? I won't be around here anyway." Suddenly, Pete's point became clear. Ray spoke as his brain processed the thought. "And if I don't eventually replace myself, the church could fall apart."

"Which is why practice number six is called *Replace Yourself*."

Practice #6
Replace Yourself

Ray was now looking to see if he could crawl up under the seat and hide there until after the game. "I'm sorry, Pete. I don't know what just happened."

"You thought I was here to fire you and that you were going home to tell your wife that you were a failure and had lost your job and your church."

"Yeah. That's pretty much what happened."

"And that's why number six is hard to do. In order to replace yourself, you have to see the good of the organization as more important than your own. You have to be able to resist that natural reaction to protect yourself and your position. But I'm really talking about a lot more than just knowing when it's time to leave. You see, for an organization to grow, you have to have great leadership. And great leadership needs to be developed through a system of apprenticing replacements and duplication."

"What kind of system?" Ray asked.

"Well, for us it's called a *farm system*. There are five other teams in our system that recruit and train players to fill the twenty-five slots we have at the major league level. Every year we have holes to fill, and the successful teams are those that fill their holes with the best talent."

"I guess it's easier to fill holes when you're paying a guy a million dollars a year," Ray said.

"Maybe. But you still have to know what you're looking for. A lot of teams have paid a lot of money for players that weren't worth it. That's why we have scouts. These guys are trained to spot talent, acquire it, and place it in the right position to be developed."

Ray thought about this for a moment. "I try to do the same thing, but it's hard to keep every area covered."

"That's why this practice can't apply just to you. In my businesses, every manager, every employee for that matter, knows that they are responsible for replacing themselves."

"How do you maintain quality if people are always replacing themselves?" Ray asked.

"First of all, I'm not talking about a revolving door; I'm talking about a process—a process of mentoring and teaching another to do what you do and to do it well. And while the other six practices will take care of quality, this practice insures that you will maintain quality over the long haul. You avoid burnout and help to prevent people from becoming entrenched."

"From becoming insiders."

"Now you're getting it. Are you sure you want to stay in church work? I can always use a guy like you somewhere."

"Funny, I was just thinking the same thing about you, Pete."

"Now *that* would cause a crisis on your board," Pete replied with a laugh.

"I don't know," Ray said as he looked up at the skybox. "It looks to me like they could get used to it."

9

MANAGING YOUR WAY TO VICTORY

Pete laughed. "Ray, I've really enjoyed our time tonight. I hope it's been helpful."

"Very helpful. But we're not done, are we? We've only covered six practices. You said there were seven."

"Yeah, but I don't think number seven is going to be as hard for you as I first thought. In fact, you've been doing it for the past couple of hours."

"Sitting in the owner's box and being waited on hand and foot? I think I can get used to practice number seven."

"Well, it's not all it's cracked up to be, and it's also not practice number seven," Pete said laughing. "Practice number seven is called *Work On It.*"

"Work on it?" Ray repeated.

"That's right. You see, Ray, most leaders see themselves as part of the system. They play a role in the organization and give everything they have to working in the system."

"And that's bad, how?"

"If a leader, you in this case, spends all of his time working in the system, then how is he going to know when the system is the problem?"

Ray knew the question wasn't rhetorical. He thought for a moment and answered, "He won't unless he works on the system, too."

"Exactly. That's why the practice is to work on it. It's what you and I have been doing tonight. We've been looking at a few ideas that can help you evaluate your organization's effectiveness. Look down there in the dugout. Do you see that guy with the clipboard?"

"Yeah. He's a pitcher, isn't he?"

"Yep. In fact, he's pitching tomorrow night. Right now he's charting the hitters in tonight's game. He's looking at the tendencies, habits, strengths, and weaknesses that will help him when he pitches. Every pitcher does that."

Ray had watched enough baseball in his life to know that major league teams kept up with every conceivable statistic. "I read somewhere that you can't manage what you can't measure. Is that what you're talking about?"

"In a way, yeah. But it's more than just measuring. It's carving out blocks of time to evaluate what you've measured to see what is working and what's not. A lot of organizations collect a lot of data, but then they file it, or worse yet, they print it in a four-color annual report and *then* they file it. The higher you are in an organization, the more important this becomes."

"Why is that?" Ray knew he should know the answer, but he didn't.

"Because when something goes wrong, your first tendency will be to blame someone. And not only will you blame them, you might fire them when in fact there was an organizational problem, not an individual problem. You can lose good people—and the confidence of your team—when that happens."

"But it's hard enough to get everything done as it is. How do you find the time to work on it?"

"You find the time to eat and sleep, don't you? *You have to see this practice as that important.* You have to eat and sleep to survive physically. You have to work on your organization for it to survive."

Practice #7
Work On It

"So I need to carve out time to evaluate and plan." Ray made a note.

"Oh," Pete added, "and don't forget to carve out time to have fun, too. Part of working on it is carving out time to celebrate your victories. That's why we give out rings and spray champagne when we win a championship. We celebrate the fact that we've won. You've got to make sure your people get to celebrate their victories..."

"Or they may join another team," Ray finished the thought.

"And that's the last thing we want to see happen," Pete added.

Ray could remember several times in the early years of Meadowland Community Church when goals were met or great plans were realized. At the time it seemed like there was no time to celebrate. There was always more to achieve and Ray would launch into the next goal. How many people had moved on to other teams because he didn't stop to celebrate with them?

⊘　⊘　⊘

"Speaking of victories," Pete broke the silence, "how about we watch the end of this game and hopefully celebrate with my team?"

"Do you think I've learned enough for one night?" Ray asked.

"You haven't learned anything yet. But you have heard a lot. Remember, these are only practices to make you more effective. They won't work in an environment that lacks clear values or hard work. But if you put them into practice, they can help you stay on track. We'll see what you've learned in a few months."

"Well, Pete, I only know one way for you to tell if I've learned anything and that's for you to come around to the church—for a little while anyway." Ray wanted to put the full-court press on Pete, but he knew better than to think he could use a hard sell on a master salesman.

"If there's one thing you can be sure of, Ray, it's that you never know where I might turn up," Pete said smiling. "After all, you never dreamed I'd be here tonight."

"I never dreamed I'd be here tonight, but I'm glad I was," Ray said genuinely. "Thanks, Pete."

Ray and Pete watched the rest of the game like any other fans. Any other fans with front-row seats and access to the home team's locker room, that is. As Ray stood waiting for the valet to return his eight-year-old minivan and, with it, return Ray to reality, he thought about what he had just experienced. So much about the evening was a surprise: the canceled meeting, the VIP treatment, and especially his time with Pete. But the biggest surprise of all was rediscovering a passion for ministry that had been suffocated under a load of complexity. Could these seven practices really make his ministry more effective?

Ray pulled out of the stadium parking lot and was once again sitting in traffic on the Meadowland Parkway. As was the case earlier, his head was filled with thoughts of the church. *Nothing has really changed*, a voice in his head told him. All the problems that had been there before would still be there tomorrow morning. As Ray thought through the challenges that lay ahead, one change had already occurred: The wrinkles on his forehead were gone and there was a slight smile on his lips.

Part
II

PUTTING THE 7 PRACTICES TO
WORK

A DILEMMA

Ray's struggle is far too common in the lives of today's church leaders. Ray signed up for ministry to make a difference. To accomplish something that was larger than himself. To see lives changed. To know that his investment would somehow count for eternity. He shared the same passion that drives most people to do what they do in ministry.

But somewhere along his journey, Ray embraced an organizational strategy that was unhealthy for his church. He woke up one morning to the realization that his church had gradually become something quite different from what he had set out to create. Ray's energy and love for ministry was being sapped by an organization that seemed to have taken on a life of its own. And it was moving in directions beyond his control. Like a disillusioned ballplayer, Ray longed for the simplicity of an earlier time—and he desperately wanted to rediscover his passion to play a game he loved.

THE PROBLEM WITH COMPETING SYSTEMS

Several years ago I (Reggie) was in the process of transferring an entire decade of important files to a new computer when I booted up my old Macintosh and found myself staring at a strange icon. Instead of the familiar smiling Mac, there was a frowning image glaring back at me. I knew enough about computers to know I was in trouble. My hard drive had crashed, and the situation was potentially critical.

Fearing that countless outlines, financial records, personal information, studies, and reports had been lost forever, I raced to the nearest computer clinic. I nervously watched as two trained technicians took turns trying to access my damaged files. When they decided to break for lunch, I remained behind, determined to figure out the problem. Unsure where to begin, I pressed the button that released the CD tray. There I discovered something I had noticed my youngest daughter playing with earlier that day. The CD in the tray contained an outdated application that I had recently discarded for a newer program; my daughter had obviously found the disc and tried to load it into my computer. When the technicians returned, they quickly analyzed the disc and found that it also contained an older version of my computer's operating system. They explained that my computer had crashed because of what they called a *systems conflict*.

The operating system is the invisible part of a computer that determines how the computer functions. It provides the computer with an internal code that drives its behavior. It sends signals to the hard disk to control how it looks and performs. If you try to boot up a computer with competing signals from two different systems, the computer becomes unstable and has a mental breakdown.

In some ways, your church is like a computer. There is an operating system that runs in the background of everything your church does. This operating system continually sends signals that basically determine how programs are designed, how ministry is organized, how communicators teach, how your target audience is reached, and how daily decisions are made. This internal code holds the key to the behavior and appearance of your entire organization. If I were to spend some significant time at your church, chances are I would learn a lot about your system. I would hear your language, listen to your questions, and watch what you practice. Sooner or later I would discover what really drives you.

Churches are notorious for creating competing systems, wherein unclear direction and conflicting information threaten to cause a breakdown and paralyze the ministry. Instead of replacing old systems, we tend to just download and add whatever is new to what already exists. Soon our capacity becomes fragmented and we find ourselves confronted with the signs of ineffectiveness: some ministries seem routine and irrelevant; the teaching feels too academic; calendars are saturated with mediocre programs; staff members pull in opposite directions; volunteers lack motivation; departments viciously compete for resources; and it becomes harder and harder to figure out if we are really being successful.

Too many churches desperately need an upgrade. They need to reformat their hard drives and install a clean system. They need to rewrite their code so everyone is clear about what is important and how they should function.

CREATING A COMMON LANGUAGE

Imagine the advantage you would have if everyone in your church operated on the basis of the same internal code. What if every volunteer and every staff member understood that certain practices were critical to the success of your mission, and that these practices were an essential part of the style and culture of your ministry? Now what if you could somehow shape these principles into words and phrases that could be effectively integrated into the language of your ministry— simple statements that would instantly remind the players on your team how and why they do what they do?

During our formative years the six people who founded North Point Community Church developed what have become known as "The 7 Practices for Effective Ministry." We had spent numerous hours writing a mission statement, clarifying our values, and drawing up diagrams of our ministry strategy. Our vision and values were basic enough that they could be framed and put on the walls of just about any evangelical church, but we felt the need to craft a series of succinct action statements that would communicate our own unique approach to ministry. We would restate our strategy in terms that would keep our leaders on the same page and help them to establish practices that would continue to replicate and infuse the DNA that made our style of ministry distinct. We were trying to establish a language that our leaders could use to coach future volunteers and staff in a unique way of doing church.

It is important to understand exactly why these practices were developed and what they are. But it is also important to understand what they are *not*. The 7 Practices for Effective Ministry are not church growth principles, but they definitely make an impact on *how* we grow.

They are not the same as our mission, but they are *strategic* in helping us accomplish our mission.

They are not the same as our values, but they determine how we *apply* our core values.

They are not theological principles, but they compliment our passion to *teach* truth with relevance.

They are not the only practices, but they have become some of the most *critical* practices for our church.

These seven practices have helped us to

...protect the simplicity of our organization.

...keep our staff and volunteers moving in the same direction.

...create environments that are focused and relevant.

...evaluate the success of our ministries and programs.

...export our style of ministry to new and existing churches.

A BRIEF DISCLAIMER

The principles and practices described in this book are not and cannot be a substitute for God's blessing or power. It is important that every church operate from a clear vision and established values that keep everyone in tune with the overall direction of the organization. It is equally important to have a clear strategy so that the church can harness its God-given resources and talent to accomplish its unique mission.

Establishing certain practices will increase the effectiveness of your ministry and programs; but vision, values, and strategy are not nearly as important to your success as being in sync with what God desires to do in your church.

practice #1

CLARIFY THE WIN

*Define what is important at every
level of the organization*

Turner Field in Atlanta stands as a monument to the fact that people will pay money to participate with a team that wins. The state-of-the-art stadium was opened two years after the Atlanta Braves won the World Series. Many who grew up watching the then-lowly Braves remember the days when a scant few thousand people would attend games in the old Fulton County Stadium and foul balls would bounce around empty seats. Today fans pack out a forty-nine-thousand-seat stadium to watch one of the most successful teams in baseball play.

Everyone wants to be a part of a winning team. But the reverse is also true: People tend to stop showing up when an organization is not winning. Nothing will empty seats faster than a losing streak. Players can complain about fair-weather fans, and owners can pour millions into slick ad campaigns, but the best way to fill seats is to *win*.

How do you know when a baseball team is winning? It's obvious. An enormous scoreboard is placed in the center of the stadium so the crowd and players can see how their team is doing. Most organizations recognize the need to have some type of "scoreboard." Public companies post third-quarter gains. Schools report their students' aggregate test scores. Television networks have their Nielsen ratings. In these scenarios the score is obvious, and there are consequences if an organization is not winning. If a company loses too much money, it goes out of business. If test scores fall below an acceptable level, a school loses its accreditation. If a TV series lags in the ratings, it gets pulled off the air.

Keeping score helps everyone involved stay informed about the condition of the organization. It's just that in some organizations it's easier to know whether or not you're winning.

How do you know, for example, if a church is winning? The very nature of what a church does makes it difficult to keep score. How do you create a scoreboard that measures intangibles like relevant teaching and changed lives?

There's an old wooden sign in the church my dad grew up in. It still hangs on the left wall behind the pulpit. Maybe you've seen one like it. The sign has slats that display numbers announcing the church's critical statistics. There is a column for "Last Week" and a column for "This Week." Every Sunday you can check out how things are progressing in three areas: attendance, the number of visitors, and total offerings. I can remember, as a kid, looking up at the numbers and thinking, *Things are getting better.* Or during some weeks, *Things are getting worse.* That sign has been hanging there for at least thirty years, but I'm not sure it truly communicates whether or not the church is actually winning.

Most churches do not have a reliable system for defining and measuring what success looks like at every level of the organization. Instead they post some general statistics that give them a vague sense of progress or failure as a church, and they go through the motions of continuing to do ministry the way they always have, productive or not.

Thus it is possible for a church to become very efficient at doing ministry ineffectively.

The church should be more determined than any other kind of organization to "clarify the win" simply because the stakes are so much higher: Eternity hangs in the balance.

HOW DO YOU MEASURE SUCCESS?

At a recent conference I was in an elevator and overheard one young pastor ask another, "How many do you average in attendance on Sunday?" and "What is your monthly budget?" Basically, the young pastor was asking his friend, "What's the score?" Right or wrong, he had a predetermined idea about how to measure success in ministry.

Too many church leaders have bought into the myth that to clarify the win means establishing attendance goals and raising a lot of money. These can certainly be indicators about the health of your organization, but strong numbers in these areas do not necessarily mean you are winning.

At North Point we have never set attendance goals, and we rarely promote financial targets. A different set of questions comes to mind when we talk about what it means to win. For example, do attendees feel comfortable inviting their unchurched friends? Are members recognizing the need to give a percentage of their income? How many individuals are successfully connecting to small groups? Do our people understand how to apply the scriptural truths we're teaching in their daily lives?

Clarifying the win simply means communicating to your team what is really important and what really matters. Asking certain questions, rewarding an individual's performance, celebrating significant outcomes—these are all part of clarifying the win. Practicing this principle means that you are intentional about defining a win so that you don't accidentally communicate the wrong win or keep your team guessing about what is really important.

The best way to leverage the collective power of your team is to make sure that everyone knows what it means to "score."

WHEN YOU DON'T CLARIFY THE WIN

Nothing hinders morale more than when team members with separate agendas are pulling against one another. When this happens, it's usually because those in charge have not taken the time necessary to clarify the win for their team.

As long as the "win" is unclear, you force your team to guess what a win looks like. One distinguishing feature that makes a church different from most organizations is the number of volunteers required to fulfill its mission. Generally, volunteers want to do what the church wants them to do, but problems occur when the volunteers try to score runs in foggy conditions: Without clear direction, they are forced to chart their own course or follow whoever seems to have the best plan at the moment.

Our experience is that most volunteers do not have personal agendas or any desire to create conflict; they just want to know where to get in line so they can help. But if they are allowed to wander in the wrong direction for long, most volunteers will ultimately give up.

Why? Because people don't like to lose—they like to win!

Every one of us has a God-given itch to belong to something that is bigger than ourselves. Volunteers need to know that their investment of time is going to make a difference. They will work hard and make incredible sacrifices as long as they know what the goal is and that what they're doing actually counts; they simply desire to find meaning and significance in their work. No one likes to go through the motions just doing menial tasks. Everyone needs to clearly understand what they are accomplishing.

Statistics suggest that volunteerism in the church is declining. One frequent question we are asked by other churches is "How do you recruit and keep volunteers?" Part of the answer is that we clarify the win. Countless individuals quit working in churches every year because they simply do not feel like they are winning.

If the win is unclear, you may force those in leadership roles to define winning in their own terms. Sometimes pastors make the mistake of thinking that they should spend more time with younger leaders and less time with stronger leaders. And it seems logical that stronger leaders should require less supervision. But when you fail to give a strong leader clear direction, you give that person permission to go in whatever direction seems right. If you don't define winning for your ministry leaders, they will define it for themselves.

Why? Because they are leaders and they're used to winning!

It doesn't take very long for leaders to take over a class, start a new program, begin an innovative ministry, and rally a crowd to follow them. They may only be ten degrees off track, but given enough time they will miss the target by miles. It's not that they are intentionally being defiant or difficult; they're just being leaders. But countless leaders have innocently sabotaged their church by leading people in the wrong direction. And the fault lies with an organization that has not been systematic about defining and clarifying what a win really is.

WINNING WITH KIDS
From North Point's Playbook

A few years into developing our children's small group program, we realized that some of our leaders were not connecting relationally with the kids. A number of our leaders were convinced they were doing a good job—since the win had not been clarified, they defined a win themselves based on what they had done in other churches.

There were some great reports. Bible stories were being taught each week. A lot of kids were attending. The activities and lessons seemed to be working. Countless details were being managed efficiently. But many of the leaders didn't feel like they were winning at all, and they were becoming frustrated. They had signed up as leaders to *connect with kids*. But many of our kids were not developing quality relationships with their small group leaders, which was a primary objective for our UpStreet Kids program. Some were attending different groups every week!

We had classes, but we didn't really have *groups*. That's because group life was just not a real priority with our leaders and parents. And so we were forced to recast the vision and clearly explain what a win looked like. This required us to redefine the roles of our volunteers, spotlight key leaders who were modeling the correct way to lead groups, and encourage parents to bring their kids to a consistent hour. We actually removed the worship and Bible story responsibility from most of the leaders so they could focus on one thing: connecting with the kids in small groups.

In the end, it took more than a year and a lot of communication with our leaders before our staff started feeling like we were really winning at UpStreet. But if we had clarified the win for our volunteers earlier, we could have avoided a lot of unnecessary conflict.

THE ADVANTAGES OF CLARIFYING THE WIN

Whenever we discuss the strategy and growth of North Point with leaders from other churches, someone always asks if we had an advantage because we started with a blank page. There are definitely some advantages when you start from scratch. We had no existing programs, minimal staff, and no charter members reminding us "how we used to do things." But having a blank page advantage is not nearly as important as having a *same page* advantage.

When you clarify the win, you help your team stay on the same page. During our first few years, the six members of our leadership team made a deliberate attempt to keep everyone on the same page. We spent agonizing hours clarifying the win in numerous areas, at times debating seemingly insignificant issues. Looking back, we are convinced that many of those decisions were strategic in keeping our staff and leaders aligned in the months and years that followed.

You see, misalignment usually happens gradually. And if it goes unchecked, it can wreak havoc on an organization. Like the wheels on a car pulling against each other, misalignment will ultimately ruin the tires, wear out the engine, and waste enormous amounts of fuel.

Misalignment is sometimes just a natural result of growth. People start showing up and they join your church with pictures of what they think church should look like. From the time they walk through the door, they start trying to conform your church to the image of their own picture. Maybe they are expecting adult classes every Sunday morning, a different style of music, or a women's ministry. Before long, these well-meaning people can begin moving your church in a different direction.

Effective leaders constantly hold up clear pictures of what the church is supposed to be, so that everyone understands what it is *not* supposed to be.

When you clarify the win, you can manage your resources more effectively. We may have had the advantage of starting with a blank page, but as our administrator Rick Holliday often pointed out, that doesn't mean we had a blank check. Rick has always done a great job of helping us figure out how to best use the limited resources we've been given to achieve maximum results. Every church must face this challenge. In the early days of a church, it means the leadership must decide what programs to start first. As the church grows and the organization becomes more complex, it means they have to decide how to divide their resources among multiple ministries.

"Whoever can be trusted with very little can also be trusted with much" (Luke 16:10). We believe this also applies collectively to the church. And yet most of us are aware of programs that have been funded for years but have made little or no real impact. That's one more reason it is important to understand what is and what is not working.

When you clarify the win, it creates the potential for positive momentum. When you have established a culture where the win is clear, the wins tend to happen more frequently. There is a lot to be said for the energetic atmosphere that happens when an organization wins consistently. Winning often triggers a chain reaction: When people learn what winning feels like, it becomes easier for them to win. That's what we call *momentum.* Momentum is actually just a series of wins; when someone says, "We need to keep up the momentum," they are actually saying, "We need to keep winning." One high school girl's basketball coach kept his team from playing official games for an entire year, because they were a young team and he didn't want them to lose so many games that the girls became "programmed" to lose.

Winning motivates a team. As long as they're winning, people will give you their time, their money, and their hearts. And when you are winning consistently, the staff and volunteers in your organization tend to...

...work harder.

...be less negative.

...trust the leadership.

...give more generously.

...stay involved.

FOUR STEPS TO CLARIFYING THE WIN

If you hope to clarify the win for your team, you have to take the time to define what is important at every level of the organization. Here are four steps to help you clarify the win and establish winning as a habit in your organization.

1. Sum up the Win in a Simple Phrase

When you formally state the win and put it in front of the entire team, it becomes a lens through which you can view everything you do. In baseball, the win is simply to "score by crossing home plate." Therefore, a good hitter doesn't step up to home plate worried about his batting average; he just wants to get on base or knock in a run. A good pitcher doesn't pitch in order to have a great ERA; he is passionate about keeping the batter from getting a hit or driving in a run. Everything that is done on the field is either an attempt to score or prevent the opponent from scoring. And each player's unique contribution is measured against what is ultimately seen on the scoreboard.

When everyone on the team clearly understands the goal, it changes how they do what they do. For example, in our InsideOut high school program a win happens "when a student has meaningful interaction and discusses life-changing principles within the context of a small group." So at InsideOut, everything that is done is measured against how it gets students to connect in small groups.

The host needs to be aware of those who need to get connected to a group and creatively communicate the importance of group life; so the win for the host happens when students choose to get connected in a group.

The worship leader should strive to create an atmosphere that prepares students to hear the message; so the win for worship happens when students participate and their hearts become open to truth.

The speaker is positioning the message to set up small group time; so the win for the speaker is measured by how well students discuss the teaching during their group time.

Those preparing refreshments help to provide a more informal time for the students to connect; so the win for those who cook is indicated by how many of the students hang around after group time and keep talking.

In the end, if students participate in an effective small group, we win; if they do not, we lose.

A KEY QUESTION
From North Point's Playbook

In our creative meetings we will sometimes ask the question, "What do we want people to walk away and do?" The answer to that question can clear up a lot of confusion about the goal of a program and force us to clarify the win. One of the first programs we started at North Point was called KidStuf. It was designed to create a shared experience for kids and parents that could be a catalyst for family time in the home. By specifically asking, "What do we want parents to walk away and do?" we were able to clarify one of the primary goals of KidStuf: to inspire parents to continue to teach their kids about character and faith throughout the week.

That decision started everyone thinking in the same direction. If the elements of our program only targeted children, then we could never expect parents to be more than spectators. Our drama, music, and video had to be created with parents in mind. Scripts and jokes had to include messages for adults. Segments of the program were designed to spotlight parents. We also had to become strategic and deliberate about providing parents tools to help them win as spiritual leaders in their homes.

Every aspect of KidStuf was reevaluated on the basis of how it engaged parents to discuss principles with their kids during the week. We became the only church around that posted signs saying, "No Drop-Offs—Kids Must Be Accompanied by Adults."

2. Keep the Win as Specific as Possible

Don't confuse defining what a win looks like with establishing a mission statement. There is an important distinction between the two. A mission statement is sometimes too general. It is more like a compass— it may be helpful to keep an organization moving in the right direction, but it does not necessarily ensure effectiveness. A mission statement is easy to manipulate and its impact difficult to measure. In fact, it is possible for any organization to be fulfilling its mission and actually losing to the competition at the same time.

When you clarify the win, it is like marking a specific destination on a map—it's easy to know when you win because you arrive at your desired destination. Maybe you've heard this business aphorism: If you aim at nothing, you will hit it every time. A lot of churches claim to reach more people every year; yet according to national statistics the church is rapidly declining in attendance and losing its influence in our nation. The fact is, a lot of churches are just not clear about where they are aiming, and so it's easy to convince themselves and everyone else they are hitting something. When you have drawn a clear and specific target, it becomes obvious when you hit or miss your mark.

Ron Blue gave us some good advice during the early days of our church. He said, "You can't manage what you can't measure." Don't make the mistake of clarifying a win in terms that are too general. When you do, you cheat everyone in your organization and you fail to establish an effective way to measure your success.

3. Restate the Win Frequently and Creatively

Once you have carefully defined a win for a department or program, you need to spend time keeping it in front of your team. It is easy to become distracted or preoccupied with secondary issues, and there will always be competing signals that sneak into your organization. So good leaders develop the habit of reminding everyone—and each other—what's really important.

Next time you're at a ball game, listen to the coaches. They are constantly instructing the players. And they encourage the players to talk to each other. That's because communication is a key to winning. Good teams communicate during every play of the game, so everybody knows what they must do at any given time.

We learned early in the life of our church how critical it was to keep the win in front of our leaders. Some of those attending assumed a win meant creating the same kind of programming they had experienced at another church. Others measured winning by how quickly we could acquire our own building. The more consistent we were at communicating the win for every program and department, the easier it was to keep our leaders and volunteers from taking unintended detours. Whatever we are using as a scoreboard needs to be in constant view of our leaders.

Countless organizations paste on their walls meaningless phrases that never stick in the hearts of their leaders because the words never become part of their everyday language. If you want your leaders to buy into it, you have to keep finding creative ways to clarify the win.

There are a number of ways a church can continually restate the win for its staff and volunteers:

- Post it on creative boards and in planning rooms as a constant reminder of what they are trying to accomplish

- Establish strategic questions that you ask at every meeting to help leaders keep thinking about the win.
- Use creative videos to document a specific win and illustrate it with comments from those who attended the program.
- Script it into your announcements and promotions so everyone can hear it.
- Brand it into an environment by creating taglines that reinforce it.

Strive to say the same thing over and over in different ways. You can't establish the win one time and expect it to stick. People need to see it and hear it constantly.

TELLING YOUR STORY
From North Point's Playbook

Every time we baptize a person at North Point, we use the opportunity to restate and communicate, in a creative way, what a win looks like to our congregation. We do this by showing a video testimony in which the person tells the story of how God's love played out in his or her life. As the individual professes faith in Christ, key people in the church are often thanked and certain environments such as Starting Point are acknowledged. These stories reinforce that the purpose for everything we do as a church is to lead people into a growing relationship with Jesus Christ.

Some people tell us they are uncomfortable and would prefer to be baptized without the video. We kindly but firmly explain that the impact of each person's story is too great not to share it with our congregation. In fact, this practice is so effective that we have built an entire event around the baptism of our children and students called the Birthday Celebration.

In fairness, I must point out that we got the idea of shooting video testimonies from a small church in our area. You should always be on the lookout for creative ways to communicate the win.

4. Meet to Clarify the Win at Every Level

Most organizations have written clever mission statements and carefully crafted their values. But few organizations have summed up in a simple phrase what a win looks like at every level of the organization. You can't stop at the top of the organization. The principle will only help you become more effective if the practice is carried through to the levels where practical ministry is happening.

It's not enough to ask, "What does a win look like for the church?"

It's not enough to ask, "What does a win look like for the student ministry?"

It's not enough to ask, "What does a win look like for the InsideOut high school program?"

You should also ask, "What does a win look like for the InsideOut small group time?"

KNOWING THE SCORE

A church really does need a scoreboard. When you establish "clarify the win" as a practice in your organization, you position everyone on your team to keep moving in the same direction. You provide a tool to measure and, therefore, manage what you do. When people know what a win looks like, they are much more likely to win. And when they start winning, chances are they will keep winning. Because leaders like to win, and they will attract others who want to join a winning team.

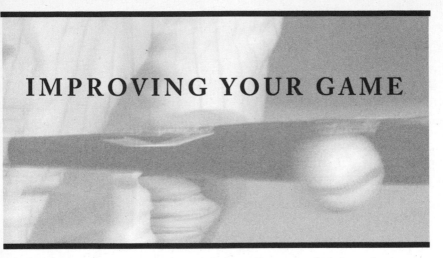

IMPROVING YOUR GAME

- What was your last "win"? How did it affect attitudes throughout your organization?

- A mission or vision statement establishes the win in a general sense, but now it is time to get specific. Practice clarifying the win for a department. Then for a program. Then for a specific staff or leadership position (e.g., small group leader).

- Name three areas where you feel it would be helpful to your organization to clarify the win. Discuss any areas in your organization where volunteers may be confused or frustrated because the win is unclear.

- Brainstorm some creative ways to communicate the win within your organization.

- Encourage every department in your organization to plan an off-site gathering to clarify the win for each of their programs.

THINK STEPS, NOT PROGRAMS

*Before you start anything,
make sure it takes you where you need to go*

I remember trying to explain batting averages to my son when he started Little League. He was convinced that anytime he hit the ball it should make his batting average go up. The problem is that a hit is not really a hit unless it gets you on base.

A hitter can slam the ball to the fence, but if it's caught in the air, he's out. And if he's out, the play is calculated negatively against his batting average. It may not seem fair to a Little Leaguer for a powerful line drive or towering fly ball to hurt his batting average. But it doesn't matter how hard you hit the ball if it doesn't get you where you need to go. The object of the game is not to hit the ball hard, but to get to home plate; and the only way to get to home plate is to go to first base. So the strategy for every batter is clear: He has to hit the ball somewhere strategically so he will have time to get to first base, or in some cases, move another runner to the next base. It may not be easy to do, but at least it's simple to understand.

Some organizations are like Little League batters. If they just hit the ball anywhere, they get excited and feel good about what they've done. It doesn't really matter if they get on base or if what they do actually gets them where they want to go. They are just trying to hit a ball somewhere. They're not necessarily thinking about home plate or the steps it takes to get there. It may be that no one in the organization has ever pointed out home plate or explained the strategy to get there. Imagine what baseball would be like if no one knew where home was. The action on the field would be chaotic and confusing. It's always difficult to have a good strategy if you don't know where you're going.

Unfortunately, churches have a reputation for doing ministry without an end in mind. They build as many rooms as possible to reach as many people as possible. They start new ministries to target a variety of different social issues. They create more programs to meet the growing needs of those who are attending. It all makes sense. It all seems right. It even feels productive. But there is no overall strategy and no runners are moving toward home. The question they should be asking is not *Are we hitting the ball?* But rather *Are we getting on base? Are we going in the right direction? Are we getting closer to home plate?*

It's possible they don't even know where home plate is!

THINKING STEPS VS. THINKING PROGRAMS

We adopted the phrase "Think Steps, Not Programs" because many of us were aware of the complexity that can develop during years of adding new programs to a church. We had all seen firsthand how competing programs can fight for budgets, calendars, and volunteers. We had learned the hard way that the gravitational pull of a church is usually toward overprogramming. During the first few years of our existence we made a deliberate decision to fight for simplicity in our church model. At times we seemed ruthless, maybe even unkind, because of our determination to say no to everything that could keep us from arriving safely at what we had determined was home plate.

There is a definite distinction to be made between a *step* and a *program*. According to the *American Heritage Dictionary*, a program is "a system of services, opportunities, or projects, usually designed to meet a social need."[1] Most churches are fairly effective at designing programs to meet needs. And the church staff usually feel like it is their responsibility to understand the needs of their congregation and community and establish the appropriate programs to meet those needs. When you "think programs," your inclination tends to be to create something in order to meet specific needs that have surfaced in your attendee base or target group.

When you "think steps" there is a fundamental difference in your perspective. Now the primary goal is not to meet someone's need, but rather to help someone get where they need to go. Notice how the same dictionary defines a step: "one of a series of actions, processes, or measures taken to achieve a goal."[2] A step is part of a series of actions that systematically take a person somewhere.

To state it another way, when you think programs you start by asking, "What is the need?" The first question is logically followed by a second question: "How are we going to meet that need?" The result is a program-oriented ministry—it is designed to meet a need.

When you think *steps* you start by asking, "Where do we want people to be?" That question is followed by a second, more strategic question: "How are we going to get them there?" The result is a ministry that works as a step—it has been created to lead someone somewhere. This way of thinking makes a lot of sense in the light of what the church is called to do.

The mission of North Point Community Church is "to lead people into a growing relationship with Jesus Christ." Our purpose is not that different from any other Christian church. We simply strive to take people from where they are to where they need to go.

First, determine where you want people to be. Then figure out how you're going to get them there. That's doing ministry with the end in mind.

THINKING STEPS FOR SPIRITUAL GROWTH

When you start thinking steps, you begin thinking specifically about how to help people move to the next stage in their *spiritual* growth. At specific critical junctures of the Christian life, this may mean a unique environment or ministry in which the church takes a hand and guides a person through.

Some of North Point's defining moments as an organization have taken place when one of our teams recognized that a spiritual step was missing from our process. For example, it's difficult for someone to jump from being a seeker to becoming a member. So Lane Jones and Sean Seay designed Starting Point, a twelve-week small group study for seekers and new believers that answers the hard questions and teaches certain foundational truths of Scripture.

But Starting Point is not just another Bible study group; it's the *only* Sunday morning adult class we offer. Starting Point exists because it helps people keep moving. It's not an end in itself. After twelve weeks, the class pushes the participants toward an ongoing community group. So for a limited amount of time our leaders hold someone's hand until he or she gets a grip on their faith; then we try to push them out of the nest and into a small group.

Often, churches have a tendency to hold so many studies or classes that they end up holding hands with their adults too long. It's like a baseball team that keeps leaving runners on first. If classes don't keep people moving, if the classes are not viewed as steps, they can actually work *against* helping people grow spiritually.

THINK STEPS FOR RELATIONAL GROWTH

On the other hand, when you think steps, not programs, you will also discover ways to help people grow in their *relationships*. Every ministry environment you create should help build bridges relationally, and thinking steps will help you leverage your environments to work in harmony with the way relationships naturally flow. For example, people are acquaintances before they become casual friends, and they must spend quality time together before intimate friendships develop.

Jesus' command was to "make disciples," and after countless hours of debate among our leadership team we have concluded that discipleship happens most naturally in the context of meaningful relationships. And we have learned that meaningful relationships are most likely to develop through the dynamic of an active small group. We are not suggesting that a small group is the only place for discipleship to occur. It just seems to us that discipleship happens best with a group of friends who are "doing life" together.

The bottom line is, we found our answer to the question, "Where do we want people to be?" And once we knew the answer to that question, we began to spend time creating strategies to lead people there. The small group became our "home plate." It was the best place for individuals to experience ministry, accountability, and life change. And so we determined not to start any new ministry or environment until we could determine how it would lead people to experience group life. We started thinking in terms of steps, not programs.

ENVIRONMENTAL RESOURCES

During our early days as a church, Andy and his wife, Sandra, visited another church, and afterward they had an interesting conversation about how the church treated people who were attending for the first time. Sandra compared the experience to inviting people into your house and then ignoring them.

Their observations sparked a lengthy discussion among our leadership team about how North Point connects with both visitors and regular attendees. As a result we came up with three categories to describe how our church environments should help strategically connect people. Just like the rooms of a house can function to help move people from formal introductions to intimate conversations, the environments of a church can work as steps to move people down a relational path to where they experience a sense of belonging and care. We believed that these environments could help people understand how to take the next step spiritually and relationally. From that point on we began to categorize every environment as a Foyer, Living Room, or Kitchen Table.

Foyer typically describes a larger environment, like a worship service, where we are sensitive to the needs of those who may be visiting for the first time. In many cases, it is an entry point for the unchurched, and it is where individuals will get their first impression of the church. The relational goal of a Foyer Environment is to make sure that people walk away and feel like *guests*. There's also a sense in which the environment strives to change their *minds* about the role of the church and, potentially, Christianity in their life.

The *Living Room* is an environment where a number of people can network and meet one another. These environments are used to host area fellowships and special events for target groups and are positioned as catalysts for relationships. When you are setting up the furniture in a living room, you want to make sure that people can sit facing each other. You want them to be comfortable and have an opportunity to get to know each other at a casual level. Our goal is for people to walk away and feel like they are *friends* with someone. It is important for people to see that there are potential relationships here where they can make significant connection. We also want their *priorities* to change and for these people to begin making decisions that keep them moving toward a right relationship with God and to consider participating with Christians in a small group context.

The *Kitchen Table* is the most intimate of environments. It is primarily what we call our small groups, or Community Group experience. This is where people should be comfortable enough to have meaningful conversations about their life and faith. Community Group is where people should begin to feel like they are *family*. It's a place for someone to experience authentic and quality friendships. Our experience also suggests that this environment is an optimal place for a person's *faith* to grow.

Once we understood the different roles of each environment, it helped us prioritize to meet specific needs and we became much more sensitive about where people need to ultimately go and what we need to do to help them get there.

HOW TO CREATE AN EFFECTIVE STEP

Andy walked into our general staff meeting one morning with a handful of construction paper. He took a blue piece of paper and placed it on the floor at one end of the room. Then he walked about thirty feet away and dropped a green piece of paper on the floor. Then he asked us a question: "If the blue paper represents groups and the green paper represents our worship service, or a foyer environment, then how are we going to get people to move from the green paper to the blue?"

Andy then selected one of our staff and asked her to stand on the green piece of paper. He then instructed her to step from the green piece of paper to the blue without touching the floor. The staff member said that obviously this was impossible. When Andy asked her why, she said, "It's too big of a step."

It was a simple illustration to show that we needed to be better at creating effective steps. Andy suggested in that meeting that for a step to be effective it had to be *easy*, *obvious*, and *strategic*.

1. Every Step Should Be *Easy*

In order for someone to be able to take the next step, it can't be too much of a jump. There have been times we were forced to create extra steps because individuals were stuck and it was just too difficult for them to take the next step.

For example, it's not easy for someone to get from a worship service of several thousand people to a small group of twelve. Even though we had set up area fellowships and other possible steps, they seemed to be too hard for a lot of people to take. So Bill Willits and the groups ministry implemented and perfected Group Link, an event that organizes into a temporary group people who are not yet involved in one of our regular small groups. It's sort of a short-term "turbo" group designed to make the process of getting connected a little easier. Group Link has served as a critical step, helping us to nearly double participation in group life in just one year.

2. Every Step Has to Be *Obvious*

Just because you have created all the right steps doesn't mean that people will automatically take them. People don't like stepping off a cliff into the dark; they have to see where the step is before they are willing to take it. People need to understand where they now are and where they need to go next. In order to make the next step obvious, leaders need to consistently explain what's important and what's next. A lack of communication about how steps work and where they are located can keep people from ever getting where they need to go.

3. Every Step Must Be *Strategic*

If a step is not strategic, then it's not really a step *to* somewhere. When Alice is lost in Wonderland she asks the Cheshire Cat, "Would you tell me, please, which way I ought to go from here?"

"That depends a good deal on where you want to get to," the Cat answers.

When Alice replies that it really doesn't matter, the grinning feline says, "Then it doesn't matter which way you go."[3]

As long as we want to lead people to a specific destination, then it is important that each step continues to move them in a clear direction toward where we want them to go. Whether it's a small group, a worship service, or a classroom, once you have defined the optimal environment where you think people can be discipled, then everything else you do should be positioned to help them get there.

A note of caution: It's too easy for an organization to develop programs that lead people in another direction or allow them to get stuck. We call that "sideways energy." It's the result of creating less-than-strategic steps that actually compete with other, more critical steps.

REPLACING A STEP
From North Point's Playbook

We actually hired and trained staff to coordinate area fellowships for married couples. These events were designed as monthly Living Rooms where couples could potentially connect and ultimately get involved in Community Groups. The gatherings happened in homes throughout the Atlanta area, and hundreds of couples attended every month. Even though by some standards these events were successful, the very staff who had created and were hired to coordinate them ultimately shut them down. The fellowships were just not as effective as they should have been at connecting people to groups.

Amazingly, this same team was primarily responsible for creating the idea of Group Link to replace the area fellowships for couples. Rather than holding on to the fellowships because they felt personally threatened, they then handed off their idea for Group Link to a different department. These people literally worked themselves out of a job! The truth is, leaders who are more focused on the mission than on the program are extremely valuable to an organization.

A STEP UP FOR THE ORGANIZATION

There are several organizational advantages to thinking steps, not programs. Here are just a few: You encourage your teams to depend on each other. You discourage individuals from becoming territorial. You erase the hard lines that exist between departments. You are more likely to uncover anything that is not working. You become more intentional about simplifying what you do. You position leaders to constantly think in terms of the big picture.

If you were to walk into a step-oriented environment or one that was designed with a programming mindset, they may feel and look very much the same. On the surface the distinction between the two approaches may not be obvious, but the difference is critical to the overall organization. A program is usually disconnected from other programs and can easily become an island unto itself. A step, on the other hand, is usually connected in an interdependent relationship to the other environments within the organization. By its very nature, a step's success is tied to the organization's success.

IMPROVING YOUR GAME

- Where is the ultimate destination in your organization for adults to experience life change? What about students? Children?

- Create a "road map" outlining the steps that lead someone new to this destination.

- Are there any steps that need to be eliminated because they don't take people where you want them to go?

- What steps may need to be created to help people get to the desired destination more effectively?

- Are there steps that take people where you want them to go but have not been clearly communicated?

12

NARROW
THE FOCUS

Do fewer things in order to make a greater impact

I tend to have a smorgasbord approach to life and ministry. Personally, I really struggle with the idea of focus. Friends who are sensitive to my dilemma suggest that I just have an "entrepreneurial" personality style. But others, including my wife, believe that I'm really an adult with A.D.D. (attention deficit disorder) and have recommended at various times that I try heavy medication. I guess the reason I'm making this confession is because I know firsthand how difficult it is to bring focus to your life. For me it is not intuitive, natural, or easy. My days can quickly become littered with unfinished projects and new initiatives.

But throughout my lifetime I have witnessed the power of uncompromising personal focus. Our world has been greatly impacted by men and women of almost single-minded determination whose contributions were defined by the passionate pursuit of excellence in a specific arena. Somewhere in their personal journey, either by accident or on purpose, these few discovered the advantage of narrowing their focus.

The sobering truth is that many of us weaken our potential by investing too much time in the areas of our lives where we have the least potential. It seems logical. Even justifiable. After all, shouldn't we work hard at improving the areas in which we are weakest?

Think about it. Does it make sense for ace relief pitcher John Smoltz to spend more time working on his hitting? His batting average *is* probably the area where he has the greatest potential for *improvement*. The problem is that hitting a baseball is *not* the area where he has the greatest potential to make an *impact*. The most important contribution that Smoltz makes to his team is his ability to pitch.

If you really want to make a lasting impact, then you need to eliminate what you do *well* for the sake of what you can potentially do *best*. As Andy would say, "Devoting a little of yourself to everything means committing a great deal of yourself to nothing." In the first three chapters of his book *The Next Generation Leader*, he unveils how critical this principle is if you hope to become a competent leader. Andy has been very deliberate to eliminate a number of "important" things so he can spend more time sharpening his skills as an effective communicator. It's no accident that thousands of adults show up every week to hear life-changing truth presented in a relevant way. This happens because Andy is uncompromising in his attempt to narrow the focus of his life. When everything else around him is growing out of control, screaming for attention, he somehow manages to stay focused on what is key for himself and this organization.

This generation has been ministered to by a number of individuals whose names are almost synonymous with their focus: Billy Graham and crusades. James Dobson and family. Bill Bright and evangelism.

John Maxwell and leadership. George Barna and research. Gary Smalley and marriage. The list goes on and on.

Your potential to make an impact with your life is directly related to your willingness to narrow your focus.

CHURCHES WITH A.D.D.

What is true for individuals is also true for organizations: There is a natural tendency to drift toward complexity. During the past decade I have developed a growing respect for the power of focus in a church. At North Point we have relentlessly pursued simplicity. A lot of churches are simply doing too much, and if you interview their staffs they will confirm this. While they are trying to reach the world, they are losing their own communities. And instead of being strong somewhere, they are weak everywhere.

The shift toward complexity is usually subtle, and it's rarely intentional. Passionate leaders introduce innovations; persistent members promote their agendas; new programs are established; traditions are born; new ideas are added to old programs. And over time the ministry begins to lose its focus, and the church becomes paralyzed by its inability to purge itself. Ministry becomes diluted because it is flowing in too many different directions. Years of adding and never subtracting have created layers of programs that all *feel* necessary.

Meanwhile, many of these churches are growing without actually *growing*. It's always dangerous to confuse activity with results. Churches may be *doing* more, but they are not reaching more people. Churches are notorious for sacrificing long-term growth for short-term progress. So much of what they do divides their resources and their focus, thus creating a barrier to real growth. They fail to understand something counterintuitive about growth: *You have to do less if you want to grow more.* And if you do more, chances are you will grow less. Here are a few of the reasons churches have drifted into complexity, making it difficult to simplify their structure.

Some churches have bought into a ministry "menu" philosophy. In the late 1980s and early 1990s, a number of experts in church growth heralded the concept of creating churches to be "one-stop shops." Every program was promoted as a potential entry point to reach the unchurched. It seemed logical, therefore, that the way to reach more people was to start more programs. The object of the game was to create as many entry points as possible—to hit as many baseballs as possible. Churches were encouraged to become cafeterias offering a large menu of programs to appeal to a variety of different tastes. Topical studies, support groups, and specialty ministries were created and funded so everyone could find something that interested them at their local church. In some cases it actually seemed to temporarily boost attendance. But in most situations this programmatic approach became extremely difficult to maintain long-term. Many of these churches are now being drained by the complexity that has resulted from a menu-ministry philosophy. Even large, successful churches are being forced to cut back staffing and programming to reprioritize.

Churches feel constant pressure to provide programs on the basis of needs. If the menu-ministry philosophy is an attempt to reach those *outside* the church, the need-focused approach is an attempt to satisfy those *inside* the church. This, too, seems very logical. If you are in ministry, you may naturally assume it is your job to meet the needs of others. There is a sense in which you are right. But you don't meet needs simply because they exist. And whether you admit it or not you already practice a selective method of meeting needs. Just try to find a church that meets everyone's needs. There is no such church, so it's logical to assume that every church has some type of filter they use to decide which needs are important enough to meet. The reality is that there are as many needs as there are people. And needs are extremely difficult to prioritize. When you try to make programming decisions solely on the basis of needs, it can ultimately lead to an unhealthy organization. If you fuel the "neediness" in your congregation, you will possibly create an inward-focused church that can potentially self-implode.

CAN YOU CARE LESS?
From North Point's Playbook

Early on our church attendance quickly outgrew our staff's capacity, and so we were forced to begin narrowing the focus of what we spent our time on. We made the same hard choices that every other church makes when confronted with limited time and resources. One of the areas that presented a difficult challenge was our approach to Care Ministry. In the early days, the vision of two incredible women, Deborah Fields and Kayron Stevens, led us to do what came naturally—meet needs. However, it quickly became apparent that we were not going to be able to meet every need that a multi-thousand-attendee church could throw at us. We knew that we would have to narrow the

> focus and, hard as it was, say no to some so that we could say yes to most.
>
> Our care director, Dave Lewis, recognized that the majority of requests we received centered on marriage issues and divorce recovery, and so we focused on those two areas. This meant saying no to a number of recovery groups and other good ideas that could have prevented us from successfully serving where we were most needed.

Individuals have been allowed to build their identity around a program, not a mission. It is normal for leaders to take pride in what they create. But it can become an unhealthy situation if leaders hold on to what they create too tightly. When individuals tie their identity to a program they've created, they lose the objectivity that is necessary to evaluate its effectiveness. And so mainstream denominations and conventional churches collectively pour millions of dollars annually into programs that should have been buried a decade ago.

There is a very fuzzy line between building your personal significance around a program and attaching your heart to a mission. Programs need to change; a mission can last a lifetime. When leaders give their heart to a mission, they hold whatever they create with open hands. Why? Because the value of a program is linked to how well it helps accomplish the mission. And a good leader is always more passionate about the mission than about the program.

Church leaders fear the fallout of eliminating certain programs. Every leader knows there is a degree of risk in eliminating any program. Someone will inevitably be angered. Pastors have been fired and churches have split over less. So who can blame a leader for cautiously considering who and how many people are going to react before pulling the plug on a program? But when a leader fears the consequences of eliminating a program more than the long-term effects of keeping a program, the result can be costly. Failing to eliminate programs that need to be purged can stunt a church's growth and tie up important resources. When a leader lacks the courage to make necessary changes, the future potential of the entire organization is put on hold.

Let's now look at some of the changes you will need to make if you are going to narrow your focus.

SIMPLIFY, SIMPLIFY

In his book *Focus*, Al Riese makes some interesting observations about the inclination toward complexity that exists within every organization. Narrowing your focus means you must *resist complexity and pursue simplicity*. Many of our staff had previously been involved with churches that were program-heavy, and we knew how quickly things could grow out of control. So we became tenacious about staying simple. In fact, you might be surprised at some of the things we *don't* do. For example, we don't have a Christian school, midweek services, men and women's ministries, a children's choir, adult Sunday school, Easter or Christmas pageants, or a recreation ministry.

It's not that anything is wrong with any of these programs. There's just not enough room in our organization to do them *and* be as effective as we think we need to be with other programs. So we require extensive documentation and layers of meetings before a new program can be started. We have mostly just said no and instead encouraged key leaders to take their ideas and start organizations outside our church. We cannot afford to implement competing systems that could make our organization unhealthy.

KILL WHAT'S WORKING

Maybe you need to eliminate what works so that something else can work better. Narrowing your focus means you *choose what potentially works best over what is presently working.* It may sound strange, but the best way to help a program work better may actually be to kill another program that is working.

Jesus highlights this principle in John 15. Although He is not referring specifically to an organization, the principle is the same. He says, "My Father is the gardener. He cuts off every branch in me that bears no fruit." Everyone understands this concept. If something isn't working, get rid of it. It's the next phrase that could revolutionize your ministry: "...while every branch that does bear fruit he prunes so that it will be even more fruitful." Pruning something that is alive—cutting off something that is fruitful so another part can be more fruitful—is painful but necessary if you want to become more fruitful.

Sometimes the healthy choice is to eliminate programs that are thriving so that something else can become healthier. Good programs can actually get in the way of other programs becoming excellent. Just because something is working doesn't mean you should keep doing it. Too many ministries are spending their best human and fiscal resources on mediocre programs. A skilled gardener learns which branches to prune and which ones to keep.

Take a close look: The program with the potential to work the best—that is, the program that will bear the greatest fruit—should be your priority.

SUNDAY SCHOOL OR SMALL GROUPS?
From North Point's Playbook

We know adult Sunday school works. You don't have to convince us. Many of the staff who started North Point worked for years in churches where we created and coordinated adult classes. We just decided that adult small groups had the potential to work *better.*

We believed that if we allowed Sunday school and small groups to coexist in our organization, it would diminish the potential of both. So we decided to put all of our eggs in the small group basket. Not only were we convinced that life change happens best in the context of small groups, but once we gave the groups our undivided attention, we discovered that they had the potential to grow at a faster rate. Today, the ratio of church attendees to those who participate in small groups is better than we ever experienced with the Sunday school model.

CREATE BRANDS

There is a fundamental question you need to answer before you can establish environments that appeal to the individuals you are trying to reach: Do your specific environments exist to promote your church? Or does your church exist to create specific environments?

The answer is critical.

(Narrowing your focus means *creating environments as distinctive brands.*)

You must decide which image you want to become primary in the minds of the target audience you are trying to reach. You have to identify for them what you are selling. Are you trying to get people to buy into your church? Or are you trying to get them to buy into an environment that is relevant?

Which one do you think is an easier sell?

This principle is understood in the marketing world. People are not looking for a General Motors car to purchase. They are looking for an SUV. Or a good deal on a sports car. They are looking for something that is relevant to their lifestyle. As they narrow their focus, they test drive various models and end up purchasing a Tahoe. Or a Saab convertible. When you ask people what they drive, they don't say "a General Motors car." They are more *specific*. The point is, they are not usually thinking in terms of a corporation; they are thinking in terms of an individual brand.

The truth is that church by its nature is a very *general* concept. And most people are not looking for a church; otherwise, churches would be full of visitors every week. What people are looking for is something that is relevant to their marriage, their family, their personal lives. What they are looking for is something that works for them as individuals. And that is something specific, not general.

One of the greatest challenges facing the church today is the need to change its image. Let's face it, everyone has some kind of opinion about church. And the people in your community have probably developed some notion or other about your church simply because it is a church. People have a perception, and even if it is false, that perception is their reality. It may be the reason they never give your church a second look. You can change the adjective in front of the word *church*. You can preach messages to redefine the meaning of *church* for all those who attend. You can spend thousands of dollars on a media campaign using television and billboards. But trying to change someone's opinion about the church in general is a hard sell.

What you *can* do, however, is change the image of your church by creating environments that are attractive and helpful for someone's season of life. When your priority is creating environments instead of marketing your church, you will make a greater impact on what your community thinks about your church.

But if you hope to start making an environment a distinctive brand you must do two things:

1. Identify a primary target group.
2. Design each environment to do one thing.

Presumably, you have limited resources and talent, so you need to first decide *who* you have the best potential to reach. Here's a news flash: You will never reach everybody, so don't try. Notice we did not say, "Don't *care* about everybody." We're just saying it's better not to try to be all things to all people. But isn't that what Paul tried to do? Yes, and we suspect he was pretty good at it. Peter, on the other hand, was better at reaching the Jews. The point is, if you try to be everything to everybody, you may dilute your potential to reach *anybody*.

You need to figure out who you are good at reaching and go for it.

Likewise, every environment should be designed to do one thing. That doesn't mean it can't do anything else; it just means that each environment should have a narrow focus. That's what makes it a distinctive brand. If you start doing too much in any environment, you may confuse your customer and you will eventually water down the environment's impact. Try to attach one word or a short phrase to every environment to "brand" its distinctiveness in the minds of your leaders. Here are a few of our environments and how we have narrowed their focus:

InsideOut—*small groups for students*
Rush Hour—*a place for students to bring unchurched friends*
Starting Point—*small groups for seekers and new believers*
7:22—*a worship experience for single adults*
Community Groups—*small groups for married couples or singles*
KidStuf—*a shared experience for parents and kids*
UpStreet—*small groups for children*

If an environment is not doing the primary thing it was created to do, then it really doesn't matter what else it does. But it's also important that you don't force an environment to do something it was not designed to do. It is okay for a specific environment *not to do* these things: be sensitive to non-Christians; resolve someone's complicated emotional issues; have in-depth Bible study; give an invitation; meet the deeper needs of Christians; reach new people; or spend quality time in worship.

For example, InsideOut is primarily a gathering of Kitchen Tables, or small groups for students, so we don't try to make it do outreach. If we were to suddenly focus on outreach, we could compromise our effectiveness at discipling students through groups. And it is critical for everyone to understand the environment's design so no one shows up with a large group of unbelieving students.

The reverse is also true. If someone shows up at Rush Hour because they hope to experience a meaningful Bible study, they will be disappointed. When you create distinct brands, you let people know what to expect, and you help leaders to meet their expectations.

KIDSTUF OR UPSTREET?
From North Point's Playbook

KidStuf, the first children's program we created at North Point, was designed so parents could participate in an environment with their kids. Instead of putting kids in an environment that was designed for adults so they would get excited about what we taught parents, we turned the idea on its head. We put parents in an environment designed for the whole family so they would get excited about what we taught their kids. The program is a fast-moving, multimedia, Nickelodeon-style presentation. It was positioned in our organization as a Foyer event.

We then created a separate environment for kids to participate in small groups and called it UpStreet. During one of our first meetings with our KidStuf and our UpStreet teams, we wrote both names on a board and asked two questions: "What should KidStuf do that UpStreet can't do?" and "What should UpStreet do that KidStuf can't do?" That meeting helped us to draw clear lines around both environments. See if you can guess which characteristics apply to which environment.

Is KidStuf or UpStreet a better place to...
...celebrate a kid's birthday?
...lead kids in worship?
...teach fun activity songs?
...communicate vision to parents?
...have in-depth Bible study?
...dialogue about personal faith?
...hold kids accountable for their quiet time?
...perform drama?
...teach kids to pray?
...spotlight special events?

By deciding what each environment was best designed to do, we enabled them to complement each other. And we created two distinct brands where everyone knew what to expect.

BUILD A TEAM OF SPECIALISTS

The reason no one has ever complained about John Smoltz's batting average is because he can throw a fastball that reaches ninety-seven miles an hour, and he has mastered a slider that makes right-handed batters tremble. Narrowing your focus means developing a team of specialists who may not do everything well, but are experts in the areas assigned to them.

It is rare in professional baseball to see players frequently change positions. They tend to become experts as either infielders or outfielders. They hone their skills to turn double plays, judge fly balls, and snag hard grounders. They learn how to field their zone of responsibility.

The average fan who has never played baseball has no idea how intricate the strategies can be for a second baseman or a catcher. There is more to think about than anyone would notice simply by watching the game. But when you narrow the focus, everyone tends to become an expert at what they do.

The same is true in an organization. When you reduce the responsibility and activity of your church, you enable your staff to become individual specialists. The goal of any organization should be to develop a team of people who are experts in their area of work. This is why some churches are able to achieve a certain level of excellence, while others continue to be mired in mediocre programming.

A more simple and focused organization allows each individual to specialize in a skill such as small group strategy, managing events, creating productions, effective communication, leading staff, coordinating hosts, writing scripts, and so on. When individuals own one primary environment or age group, it forces them to dig deeper and discover more. When they do more of the same thing, they just get better at doing it. They will tend to generate more ideas, create better resources, and impact more people than they would if they have too much varied responsibility. Experts tend to implement strategies that are much more effective, so churches that breed specialists have a clear advantage over churches that are full of generalists.

NARROW IS THE PATH

When you apply the principle of "narrow the focus" to your environments, you will discover a number of advantages almost immediately.

The more you focus each environment, the *greater the relevance*.
If you have a roomful of high school believers, it is much easier to target your communication to teach something applicable than if you had a room filled with both believing and unbelieving high school students.

The more you focus each environment, the *better the connection*.
When an environment is focused on a specific season of life, the potential for individuals to network relationally always increases. Every time you narrow your focus, you magnify the level of the relationships. For example, teens will connect, but teenage girls will connect *better*, and ninth-grade girls will connect *even better*.

The more you focus each environment, the *higher the quality*.
A lot of churches struggle to achieve excellence because they are just doing too much. When there is less to do, you can do whatever you do more efficiently. When churches visit North Point, they often remark on the level of quality they see in a given environment. But when we explain to them what we *don't* do, they usually admit they could do what we do if that's all they did.

The more you focus each environment, the *stronger the impact*.
Focus is why a river has more force than a swamp. Focus is the reason you can do surgery with a laser, but not a flashlight. It's the reason some churches effectively influence their communities and others don't.

TOO TOP-HEAVY TO MAKE THE TURN?

It's important to understand how "narrow the focus" is different from the other practices we have discussed thus far. "Clarify the win" means evaluating and defining what is really working. It is an important practice to familiarize everyone with what success looks and feels like. "Think steps, not programs" is about identifying and implementing programs which actually function as steps that move people in a strategic direction. "Narrow the focus," on the other hand, is about deciding to do less in order to be more effective. It calls leaders to develop the skill and willingness to eliminate certain programs so other programs can become stronger. It suggests that you create brands that are distinct and target a specific group. It requires the creation of a "not-to-do" list in order to protect the organization from the draining effects of complexity.

There is something about living in complexity that blinds you over time. But when you go back to what is simple, you begin to realize how things were meant to be. It's like leaving the city and driving into the mountains: When you eliminate the distractions, it's easier to focus on what matters. We often find ourselves in conversations with frustrated staff members from other churches. They know they do too much, but they don't know how to stop. And they are victims of a system that is so complicated, they are wasting their best talent.

Some churches are so loaded down with unnecessary baggage, they can't make the turn fast enough to keep up with a changing culture. They are getting behind because they're loaded down with stuff that is just not as important as they think it is. Even when they admit that it feels too complicated, they are still somehow convinced that it is all very necessary. They don't know how to go back. And no one will give them permission to stop doing anything. They are losing their potential to make an impact because of the complexity of their organization. Today's church needs wise and courageous leaders who will simplify their activity and refocus their mission.

REFOCUS YOUR MISSION

Whenever a church decides to narrow its focus, it should be in the context of our calling to lead people to follow Christ. For that is how the church is primarily different from every other organization. We are not in the business of education, social reform, or political revolution. Any of these issues can potentially dilute the effectiveness of the church. We could spend hours debating to what degree the church should be involved with a number of issues. But let's stay focused. History proves that it is too easy for the church to get distracted. Our business is to provide hope and salvation for the human heart. And face it, that's a mission that definitely deserves your undivided attention.

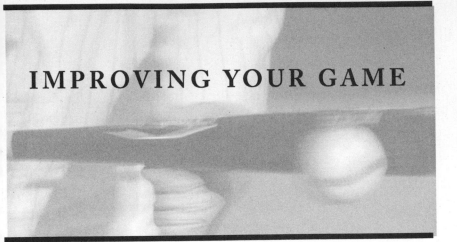

IMPROVING YOUR GAME

- Identify any programs in your organization that are providing the same step. Which one has the greatest potential to become more effective if you eliminate the other?

- Is there an effective program that you should eliminate because it is preventing a more important program from becoming more effective?

- Are there activities or programs that have become barriers to excellence in your organization?

- Create a "not-to-do" list outlining programs your organization *shouldn't* do. In other words, decide now what you will never do.

- Try to attach a word or short phrase to each of your environments to "brand" its distinctiveness in the minds of your leaders.

- Assign each person on your team to describe, in one sentence each, every other team member's primary contribution to the organization. Share and discuss each list.

practice #4

TEACH LESS FOR MORE

Say only what you need to say
to the people who need to hear it

I have notebooks full of sermon outlines and Bible study notes that I wrote down while growing up in church. I'm sure my old notes still have some value, but I don't ever really use them. When I attend conferences, the speakers usually cover so much material that I leave with only a vague, general feeling of conviction—I'm never really sure what I should specifically *do*. The fact is, I have accumulated a lot of knowledge in my life, very little of which is actually helpful on a practical level.

Every day each of us is bombarded with countless suggestions, opinions, and ideas. Hundreds of self-help books are published every year, offering similar advice on how to deal with the same problems. There are multiple steps to every goal and endless lists of things that we need to learn how to do better. Our lists have sub-lists. We may even find ourselves paralyzed to inaction because we don't know where to start. As we try to absorb more and more facts in this information age, we may, in fact, find we are able to know and achieve less.

INFORMATION OVERLOAD

My dad is primarily responsible for my love of baseball. He coached me during my Little League years, and I can still remember our hours together on the field, working through drills. There were certain basic skills that I spent the majority of my time learning, but there was also a language I gradually picked up that helped me learn how to play the game. Many of these words and phrases are etched into the minds of people who have never played America's favorite pastime:

"Keep your eye on the ball."

"Use two hands to make the catch."

"Hit your cut-off man."

"Keep the ball in front of you."

"Just make contact."

Most of the things my coaches told me were designed to help me improve in one of four areas: hitting, throwing, catching, and running. I'm sure there were a lot of different things I could have learned about baseball, but my time was spent learning how to do a *few* things. Can you imagine coaches spending practice time discussing the history of baseball with their players? Or giving a detailed lecture about how scoreboards work or the best kind of grass for sodding an infield?

I'm sure my dad could have taught me a lot more about the game, but he taught me only what I needed to know to become a better player. That's what coaches are supposed to do. A good coach focuses on the fundamentals of the game. A good coach teaches you how to hit a fastball, run the bases, catch a fly ball, field a grounder, and throw someone out. And they don't waste time on anything that really doesn't help you improve your game.

But what if I decided to download years of baseball knowledge to my wife? I could make flash cards for each critical phrase or draw detailed diagrams. I could list for her every scenario you may face as a player and explain what you should do in each situation. How quickly do you think she would master this knowledge when it has no relevance to her everyday life? Let's face it. You don't learn something until you really *need* to know it. And the greater the need, the higher the interest and the potential to actually learn.

For example, I never became interested in apologetics until I had to deal with agnostic professors. I never listened to advice about marriage until after my wedding day. I never read books about parenting until my kids were born. I never learned how to do graphic design until I had to lay out my own presentations. I never compared different kinds of motorcycles until I decided to purchase one. How much do you think I would have learned about any of these things before I felt the need to learn?

Most people don't learn just so they can know more; they learn when they need to know something. So communicators and teachers have a critical responsibility: They must make sure they know what people really need to learn. And in some situations, they need to spend time making sure people understand *why* they need to learn something. It's the only way a teacher can expect any student to learn. Yet too many churches are teaching "baseball lingo" to people who really are not interested in the game. Or in some cases, they are trying to explain baseball history to someone who just wants to know how to get a hit and get on base.

LESS IS MORE

When we say, "Teach less for more," we mean that you should rethink what and how you communicate to your team. If "narrow the focus" suggests that you make a stronger impact when you *do* less, "teach less for more" implies that you can drastically improve how much people learn if you *teach* less.

That doesn't necessarily mean that you say fewer words, but rather, that you narrow the scope of what you teach to cover less information. In some cases, you will actually say more about fewer things. But here's the key: The things you choose to teach should be limited to those things that your people most need to hear—in other words, the core principles most appropriate to your target audience. These are what we refer to as the "irreducible minimums" of learning.

John Coné, the vice president of the Dell Computer Corporation's Dell University, has said:

> The teaching philosophy of most companies today is similar to that of the schools I went to—lots of people sitting in a classroom, with an expert up front telling you things. I've always thought that if that was the natural way for people to learn, we ought to see four-year-olds on the playground spontaneously forming themselves into rows. The natural way to learn is simply to be who we are and to do what we do. Kids learn by doing things. And they learn new things when they need to know them.[1]

If you are responsible for training in your organization, you must learn to prioritize information. You have to take a look at what your target audience needs to know and separate what is most important from what is just interesting. Why? Because you have a limited amount of time to communicate with these people. And when it comes to information, all knowledge is *not* equal. There are facts that would be nice to know, and then there is information that is really interesting. But much more important, there's a body of knowledge that is critical for certain individuals in your organization to understand.

Good teachers begin by identifying what is most important for their students to know.

TEACH WITH THE END IN MIND

We have taken thousands of leaders through a mental exercise that helps explain the idea of irreducible minimums. Andy introduced the idea at our GrowUp conference several years ago.

Imagine this. You are about to retire from student ministry. Your pastor has just given you a gold watch. He asks you to stand at the front to allow people to come up and thank you for all your years of dedication. While you stand there, three teenagers walk up to you and thank you for the difference you've made in their lives. Each finishes with this phrase: "One thing I learned from you that I'll never forget is…"

How would you want them to finish that sentence? Take a minute and complete that phrase for yourself. Write down at least three different things that you would love to hear from students who have come through your ministry. Not three experiences, but three things you have taught that you hope they never forget.

You have to *teach with the end in mind.* "Think Steps, Not Programs" answers the question "Where do you want people to be?" whereas "Teach Less for More" answers the question "What do you want people to *become?*" Your ministry needs to paint a clear picture of what you hope a child will become by the time he or she transitions to middle school. You also need to have a good idea of what students should understand when they start high school, when they graduate to college, and so on. When you have established a vision for each stage of a person's life, you have established a way to measure what you teach. This also provides an image for you to use to keep your teachers on the same page. And when you filter everything you teach through this lens, it becomes much easier to decide what you should say, as well as what you should not say.

When you teach with the end in mind, you are forced to prioritize what you teach. That may include which parts of the Bible you teach. Maybe you feel that you are obligated to teach *all* of the Bible to a specific age group. Don't try to do it. You cannot effectively cram *all* of the Bible into a few hours each week for a few years. That would be information overload—you would be teaching *more* for *less*.

Please consider the following observations about teaching Scripture. Read these *carefully* before accusing us of heresy. The "Teach Less for More" practice is based on three premises. The first:

All Scripture is equally inspired.

We have summed up our entire doctrinal statement with one sentence: "We believe that what the Bible says is true *is* true." In 2 Timothy Paul writes that "all Scripture is inspired," and he goes on to suggest that because it is inspired the Bible should be the basis for everything we teach. We just don't think it is possible to teach *everything* in the Bible to every age group. So consider the next premise:

All Scripture is not equally important.

An extremely questionable statement? Think about it for a minute. We are not suggesting that any one passage is any less inspired than any other; we're just suggesting that some truth is more important than other truth.

Isaiah 40:22 says, "He sits enthroned above the circle of the earth." This is an inspired passage. Some believe this description of a spherical earth intrigued a man by the name of Christopher Columbus. Now consider another passage where the Bible says something about the world: "For God so loved the world that he gave his Son" (John 3:16). Both passages are equally inspired. But do you really think both passages are equally *important*? If you had only one opportunity to teach a group of kids about one of those two passages, which one would you choose?

Not convinced? Check out Matthew 22:37–38. When Jesus emphatically describes a specific commandment—"Love the Lord your God with all your heart and with all your soul and with all your mind"—to be "the first and greatest commandment," He clearly establishes the fact that some truths are more important than others. And this leads us to a third logical premise:

All Scripture is not equally applicable.

If you've worked with different age groups, you know this is true. There may be key truths that are important to teach at every stage, but there are others that are just not as applicable for a specific age group. That's the reason we don't teach preschoolers about the "beast" described in Revelation. Or we don't tell our kindergarten groups the details about David and Bathsheba. It makes more sense to help the young kids grow in their understanding of God as a heavenly Father, and Jesus as someone who wants to be their friend forever. Imagine talking to fifth-graders about the genealogy of the Bible. It's just too much. It's not something that would even make sense in their world. But with the hormones raging in the teen world, we may do an entire series on David and Bathsheba or Joseph and Potiphar's wife.

The goal of "teach less for more" is to identify and package a handful of must-know, can't-be-without, age-appropriate principles for each target group. If you work with high schoolers, for example, you need to be realistic about how much time you will actually have with them before they graduate. If yours is like most student ministries, you will spend about one hundred and fifty hours with those who come to your programs consistently. So the question is, What are you going to say in the time you have?

You need to streamline your curriculum. This is true for teachers of every age group. Some things are just more significant than others. Of course, you should never compromise the stories or principles that reinforce the essentials of faith. Scripture that helps someone understand salvation, grace, faith, and other critical aspects of the gospel should definitely be a priority. The key is taking the time to decide beforehand what the *big* issues are for each group and then establishing them as your irreducible minimums.

Remember, these carefully selected truths are not *all* that is important, but what are *most* important for your target audience to know.

THE PRINCIPLE AT WORK

Several years ago I sat in a room with parents and teachers to rethink what we needed to teach our children. At the time I had four children in their elementary school years. As we searched through different curriculums, I kept looking for a printed master plan, something from each publisher that would answer such questions as "What do we hope children will understand when they grow up?" and "What are the biblical truths we consider to be critical for this age group to embrace?"

Many curriculums are arranged thematically. Some attempt to take a class through the entire Bible chronologically over a couple of years. Every curriculum tries to be age-appropriate, and each publisher strives to make sure theirs is biblically sound. The problem is that too few have been developed with an end in mind. When you look at a typical publisher's "scope and sequence" and review the curriculum's multiple-year track, you should always ask yourself one key question: "What will this curriculum help a child to ultimately become?"

Every class, every teacher should be equipped with a master plan that specifically identifies what they want someone to become as a result of what they teach. Teaching without a master plan is like choosing random puzzle pieces from different boxes and trying to force them to fit together—you will never have a big picture for staff, leaders, volunteers, and even parents to see and work toward.

THE LUKE 2:52 MODEL

The concept of Luke 2:52 has always been a challenge for me as a leader and a dad. The concept that Jesus grew up "in wisdom and stature, and in favor with God and men" provides a clear model for spiritual growth. Shortly after my children were born, I adopted it as a personal goal for them and any other children I was responsible to lead. It is a short, simple passage but it answers the question "What do I want my children to become?"

Based on this verse, we have divided a child's spiritual growth into three categories: wisdom, faith, and friendship. And we have determined that three specific issues are critical to helping a child become a healthy believer:

1. The ability to make wise decisions based on the truth of Scripture.
2. A willingness to put their faith in God through every situation of life.
3. Their demonstration of love and kindness to the people in their world.

These three concepts have been crafted into concise statements that we use to challenge parents and leaders. We want every kid to grow up and come away from UpStreet or KidStuf and say:

"I need to make the *wise* choice!"

"I can *trust* God, no matter what!"

"I should treat *others* the way I want to be treated!"

These phrases provide the filter for everything we teach to children. We created a curriculum called 252Basics that organizes Bible stories, scriptural principles, drama, and creative lesson plans around these three concepts. From the moment a child walks through the door, every activity reinforces one principle over and over. Our Bible story time always positions Scripture as a source of *wisdom*. The worship always emphasizes the power and love of God as one we can *trust*. Small groups allow an opportunity for kids to be with *friends*, to dialogue about their faith and encourage each other.

Here's the point. When you decide what you want a child to become, it changes the way you teach. And when every parent, teacher, and small group leader gets on the same page that child has a much better chance of becoming what you hope they will become. You teach less and get more.

IRREDUCIBLE MINIMUMS
From North Point's Playbook

Our goal is simple. We identify a set of essential truths for every age group. We then give our leaders and staff permission to teach these principles over and over again for the sake of learning and applying them. Here are some examples from our various age groups.

We want our preschoolers to walk away knowing that

1) "God *made* me"; 2) "God *loves* me"; and 3) "Jesus wants to be my *friend* forever."

We want our children to walk away knowing 1) "I need to do the *wise* thing"; 2) "I can *trust God* no matter what"; and 3) "I should *treat others* the way I want to be treated."

We want our middle school and high school students to graduate knowing 1) "I can *trust God* with every area of my life"; 2) "When I see as *God sees*, I will do as *God says*"; 3) *"Purity* paves the way to intimacy"; 4) "My *friends* will determine the *direction* and *quality* of my life"; 5) "In light of my past experience and *future dreams,* what is the *wise* thing for me to do?"; 6) "I must *consider the interests of others* ahead of my own"; and 7) "Maximum *freedom* is found under *God's authority."*

The "teach less for more" concept can also be applied beyond age groups. For example, we have recently had conversations about defining the irreducible minimums for our staff, for small group leaders, for leadership, etc.

FOUR STEPS TO TEACH LESS FOR MORE

To teach less for more involves a four-step process.

1. Decide *What* You Are Going to Say

So many teaching resources are now available that it's possible for churches to teach for years and never repeat anything. Therefore, our leaders are responsible for determining early on what is important for our people to learn. Each department has spent time zeroing in on the primary core of information to be conveyed to their particular season-of-life group. By targeting the needs of each specific age group and then prioritizing our teaching to address those needs, we have established the irreducible minimums for every department.

2. Decide to Say *One Thing* at a Time

The "teach less for more" concept not only means we prioritize the core of information we try to teach, but that we also say less each time we meet. Traditional preaching tries to squeeze as much information as possible into every message, with alliterated lists designed to instill several life principles each week in the hearts and minds of listeners. The problem is that people do not learn that way.

Too much information may, in fact, have a canceling effect—that is, multiple ideas or concepts can actually compete with each other for the listeners' attention and retention. If you introduce a thought then quickly jump to a different thought, you now are competing with your first thought. And with every additional idea you introduce, you diminish the effectiveness of the prior ideas you have already presented.

Our preschool and children's directors recently read *The Tipping Point*, in which author Malcolm Gladwell makes several interesting observations about what make messages "stick" with audiences. In a chapter called "The Stickiness Factor," Gladwell illustrates the canceling effect in terms of television advertising:

> According to a study done by one advertising research firm, whenever there were at least four different fifteen-second commercials in a two-and-a-half minute commercial time-out, the effectiveness of any one fifteen-second ad sinks to zero.[2]

On the other hand, we have discovered that when people walk away from one of our services clearly understanding a single principle, they are much more likely to *apply* that principle in their daily lives.

TAKE THEM ON A JOURNEY
From North Point's Playbook

When it comes to the average Sunday morning sermon, most communicators seem to think that more is better. More points, more stories, more verses, more of everything. And so instead of going home with a lot of good ideas, the average listener often walks away with none. Choosing instead to teach less for more, Andy Stanley sees his role as that of a guide inviting people on a journey—a journey that leads to one life-changing principle.

The task is to engage the congregation and take them on an expedition to discover and take home that life-changing principle. Music, drama, and video are among the elements used as vehicles for the journey. These elements should deliver a message that is headed in the same direction as the sermon.

In preparation for Sunday morning, creative planning revolves around a "written brief," or the main point we are trying to get across to the audience. Predetermining the bottom line and putting it in writing for everyone involved helps to ensure that every creative component will complement that principle. We have found that it is too easy to waste enormous creative energy and frustrate talented thinkers when they have no clear bottom line to keep them on the right track.

By keeping her team focused on a single bottom-line

idea, Julie Arnold, our director of worship service programming, is able to craft the entire service around getting people to remember one thing. This increases the "stickiness factor," giving a well-crafted bottom-line principle a much better chance to stick in the mind of each listener.

Focus on just one truth or principle and you enhance the potential of every listener to really "get it."

3. Decide *How* You Are Going to Say It

Communication is really about engaging the mind and the heart of the listener, and so it is important to appeal to a variety of learning styles. So we spend time working on a variety of ways to enhance the message. There is nothing unique or distinctive about the tools we use—drama, videos, music, humor. Anything that will amplify and clarify what we are trying to say. What's important is that everything *in fact* complements the bottom line. For example, we have discovered that we can have so much going on that it actually confuses a younger audience. And when an audience gets confused, they disengage.

4. Say It *Over* and *Over* Again

What is worth remembering is always worth repeating. Repetition is not bad. Repetition is how we learn. One of the myths that teachers buy into is the idea that you have to keep a student's interest by constantly introducing them to new information. As Andy would say "Presentation, not information, engages a student's imagination." The more creative you are with your presentation the more effective you will be in communicating relevant information. You can listen to ten different versions of the "Good Samaritan" story and they can all teach you about God's unconditional love. But the one that will stick with you will be the one that was packaged in an engaging and relevant way. We already hear the same things over and over. The problem is not finding new information, but in making a better presentation of what is timeless, so that it will never be considered irrelevant.

WHY CHURCHES TEACH MORE FOR LESS

There are a number of reasons churches find it difficult to establish "teach less for more" as a practice in their organizations.

It's easier to teach more for less than it is to teach less for more. Conventional methods are just easier. When you teach a list of multiple points, you can spend a few minutes developing each idea. But if you teach one principle, you have to creatively amplify and explain it until it is thoroughly understood.

The context of ministry tends to be more demanding than the content. Sunday comes every week, and there are a lot of "urgent" needs screaming at a leader. Most of it has to do with the *context* of ministry. You have to select music, arrange the room, coordinate technical needs, find more leaders, and so on. But what if you could spend at least an equal amount of time each week on what is actually to be taught? In fact, the context should become secondary to the content. Everything about your environment—the songs, the décor, the video, the signage—should reinforce the content.

They have bought into a myth about "going deep." Some teachers will play the "need to go deeper" card to justify their style of teaching. Too many churches have been turned into classrooms. Some leaders have been programmed to teach that way, while others *think* they are going deeper, when in reality their lessons are going over someone's head. When you teach less for more, it doesn't mean you water down your message; it just means that you *focus*. Like food or drink, a message that is concentrated is much stronger than one that is diluted.

They worry about not having enough to say. Every teacher fears being in front of an audience and running out of material. Saying more about one thing requires more study, but your goal is not to fill your time slot with plenty of words. The object of communication is not to cover a lot of material but, rather, to make sure people learn. As Howard Hendricks would say, "If the student hasn't learned, the teacher hasn't taught."

They fear they will leave something out. The temptation is to explain everything about a subject so that no one misunderstands. When teaching about God's grace, for example, there is a tendency to make sure everyone knows where you stand on God's judgment. The concept of "teach less for more" suggests that if you have a master plan you will ultimately say everything you need to say on a subject. It's okay if you don't cover every side of an issue during one sermon. Again, in your attempt to explain everything, your audience may not understand anything.

What they teach is predetermined by entities outside their ministry. When I was in my twenties, I worked with teenagers. The curriculum we were given by our denomination seemed outdated and irrelevant, so I decided on my own to change it. A few weeks into the new program I received a phone call from a concerned father. While trying to justify the switch in materials, I remember finally saying, "The main reason is that all the students just think it's boring!"

I'll never forget the father's response. He said, "What does *that* have to do with anything? It was boring when *I* grew up using it."

Soon after, I got a phone call from our denominational curriculum representative.

Unfortunately, what you teach may be influenced by a number of outside forces. And my experience has been that denominations can provide some great resources. But sometimes their approach seems threatened by newer and more relevant methods. Just remember, the denomination is not directly responsible for the spiritual life of the individuals who attend your church. *You are!*

Once you have defined the irreducible minimums of your ministry, you must decide what resources best fit with what you are trying to say. Don't let someone else sell you something *they* want you to say.

From time to time, people ask us, "What curriculum do you use?" A better question is "What do you teach your kids?" If you don't know the answer to the second question, it really doesn't matter what curriculum you choose.

They are confused about the difference between information and application. The first time I spoke in church was a defining moment for me. I received several compliments from those who listened, and at lunch I was fishing for a response from my dad. I'll never forget what he said: "It was pretty good, but next time when you're speaking, you need to think about all those people who live in the real world." It stung, but it was true.

People who live in the real world have a way of seeing through empty clichés and superficial principles. It's easy to speak on any subject; if you do enough research you can come up with plenty of material. But people are not going to listen to you if you're teaching something they really don't need.

When you're looking over your lesson or sermon notes, the question to ask yourself is *not...*

Is it true?

Is it interesting?

Is it creative?

Is it passionate?

Is it entertaining?

Instead, ask yourself, Is it *helpful*? If it isn't helpful, then it isn't relevant.

My son's first year in high school was an education for me. That first winter we studied through the night for a literature exam that counted for 25 percent of his final grade. I was drilling my son on a Shakespearean drama when, about one o'clock in the morning after hours of trying to guess what he needed to memorize, he looked at me and said, "Why do I need to know this?" I could tell he was frustrated, and so I gave him the classic ten-minute fatherly speech about the benefits of education and that he was learning to learn.

My son was unimpressed. "Do you know what I *really* need to know?" he asked.

A little surprised that there was actually something he was interested in learning, I replied, "What do you need to know?"

Then he smiled and said, "I need to know how to dance. Homecoming is in a few weeks, and I think that's something that is important to know."

I have thought about that conversation a lot over the past few years. People attend churches every week and listen to someone teach Shakespeare when what they really want to know is how to dance. Kids show up at our programs and, even though they never say it aloud, they are dealing with a mess at home and are hoping someone will teach them the right moves. Our teenagers are facing incredible temptations and personal issues, and they come to our church because they need to know how to take the next step without tripping over their own feet.

Shakespeare may be interesting, but for most of us it is not very helpful. People need teachers who will reprioritize what they are communicating. They need leaders who will take them by the hand and teach them how to dance.

IMPROVING YOUR GAME

- Identify a handful of must-know, can't-be-without, age-appropriate principles (irreducible minimums) for each target group in your church—married adults, high school students, preschoolers, etc.

- State your irreducible minimums in a creative way that your leaders and volunteers can remember.

- Practice crafting in a memorable way the "bottom line" you hoped to communicate in a recent message or lesson.

- Evaluate a recent worship service and identify which elements (e.g., music, drama, announcements) did not complement the focus of the message. Remember, the goal is for everything to reinforce the bottom line. If you were approaching the same service this Sunday, what could you change to effectively teach less for more?

- Brainstorm some new tools or creative elements you can use to enhance your productions or environments.

14

LISTEN TO OUTSIDERS

*Focus on who you're trying to reach,
not who you're trying to keep*

As James Earl Jones intones in his famous soliloquy from the movie *Field of Dreams*, "The one constant through all the years has been baseball. America has rolled by like an army of steamrollers. It has been erased like a blackboard, rebuilt and erased again. But baseball has marked the time." Through the past one hundred and fifty years, America had endured a civil war, two world wars, strong economies, weak economies, and even a Great Depression. But there had always been baseball.

Until 1994. The year of the strike.

That year baseball insiders were busy doing what insiders in any organization naturally do—discussing, debating, and negotiating with each other. The collective bargaining agreement between the players' union and the team owners had elapsed, and the season had begun without a new contract in place. Every decision made during the spring and summer months that followed reflected the interests of those who profited monetarily from baseball, and America learned that when it came to their beloved game, there were two groups of people. There were the insiders: the owners, the players, the lawyers, and the unions. And there were the outsiders: the fans.

Every once in a while, the media would interview a disgruntled fan who voiced the discontent of the people. Occasionally, someone representing the owners or the players would address the public and talk in exalted terms about the best interests of baseball and its fans. But the truth is that the fans were on the outside of the debate, and there wasn't a fan in America who wanted a strike.

There were legitimate complaints on both sides of the bargaining table, and there were players and owners who genuinely didn't want a strike. But in the end, a labor stoppage could not be averted. And although millions in revenue from ticket sales and television contracts were lost, the real losers were the fans. The outsiders.

For the first time in a century, there was no World Series.

INSIDER THINKING

It's easy for the needs or interests of insiders to ultimately drive the priorities of any organization. It's just the natural tendency of any group to become insider-focused. If you are surrounded long enough by people who think like you think, you will become more and more certain that's the *best* way to think. Over time you find yourself inclined to completely disregard the concerned voices of those positioned on the *outside*.

Shortly after moving to Atlanta, Debbie and I decided we needed a new car. So we spent an entire Saturday, with all four of our elementary-age kids, going from dealership to dealership in the metro area. The ordeal was so draining, we almost decided to take our bicycles out of storage and wait another year before even thinking about car shopping again. Everything I despised about trying to buy an automobile had come flooding back.

The rote discourse that begins, "We have a special this weekend only."

A salesman I have never met before pretending he's my best friend—until he finds out what I can *actually afford.*

Being pressured to make a decision that I really don't want or need to make.

Arguing over an inflated price tag, when all I really want to know is the bottom line.

At one dealer, I walked up unnoticed behind two salespeople and overheard one ask the other, "How many did you get today?" I remember thinking, *I don't want to get "got." I just want somebody to help me.*

You may say that's just the nature of buying and selling cars. But what we discovered at the last dealership that day was a refreshing surprise. First of all, we actually made it to the door of the showroom without getting ambushed by an overzealous salesman. I remember stepping into a large room with computer terminals lined against the walls. There was a central visitors desk with a sign that read, "Let us know if you need assistance." In the back corner was a glassed-in playground for the kids, staffed with a babysitter! On the other side was a small café that provided snacks and drinks. We gave our name to the host at the visitors desk, checked our kids in at the playground, and sat down at a touch-screen computer. We typed in our price range and the model we were interested in, and the computer printed a list of compatible cars with their pictures and prices. The printout even showed us where the cars were located on the lot. Soon someone called our name and we met the salesperson assigned to us.

After introducing himself, the salesperson said something astonishing:

"Our company goes out of its way to hire people who are *not* professional car salesmen. The majority of us are not professionals. This is my first job selling cars. I'm pretty much just like you.

"There's something else you need to know. The prices shown on the stickers *are the bottom line*, we haven't built in inflated costs, so that also means there's *no negotiation*. We'll just keep working with you till you're comfortable with what we offer."

When I left that day, I didn't feel beat up or used. No one had manipulated or pressured me. And I came really close to buying a car.

THINKING OUTSIDE

Most car dealerships have one priority: to sell a car. But this one had a different priority: to help a customer. I imagine somebody stood up in a meeting one day and said, "Guys, we have been in this business for so long, we've forgotten what it's like to have to buy a car. We need to *rethink* how we are treating the customer and remember what it is like to walk in *their* shoes."

Some of us have been in church for so long, we've forgotten what it's like to never attend. We have believed what we believe for so long, we don't know how an unbeliever thinks anymore. And when the average person shows up at a church for the first time, too often he or she feels like the customer who walks onto a new car lot. In many cases the person leaves feeling suspicious, pressured, and even manipulated.

North Point Community Church was established in part to be an alternative to what most people experience at other churches. We created a church with *outsiders* in mind. After all, Atlanta didn't need another church. There are more churches than Waffle Houses in Atlanta, and if you've ever been to the South, you know that's a lot of churches. Still, most people in Atlanta weren't *going* to church. So we made it our goal not to reach those who were already going to church, but to reach everyone else.

Consider these statistics. According to Barna Research about 100 million Americans of all ages are unchurched. George Barna claims, "If all of the unchurched people in the United States were a nation of their own, they would be the eleventh most populated country on Earth."[1] Now that's a lot of untapped outsiders.

You probably drive by them every Sunday on your way to church. You also pass a number of churches along the way, most of which are not filled to capacity. So if a large portion of the population is not going to church and the majority of churches are not full, that means there's a lot of room in the churches that exist for people who are not going. *And yet most churches now being built are patterned after churches that already exist.*

Our point is that churches all over this country are striving to reflect the interests, values, and needs of people who are already attending church. The church today is primarily characterized by insiders reaching insiders.

Read or study any report about church attendance in America. They all suggest the same thing. Each generation is more skeptical and less likely to attend. Most experts believe that 70 percent of college students who have grown up in church will drop out when they go to college. Attendance is declining and those on the outside seem to have a growing indifference toward what the church has to offer. Millions of outsiders see what the church does as being irrelevant, and yet most churches continue to do business as usual.

Just for logic's sake, let's apply some common business sense to the situation. Would it make more sense to try and capture a market that is already saturated, where the majority of customers are presently using your product? Or would you go after the 100 million people who are not using your product? You can either continue to reach the customers that have already been reached, or you can attempt to reach new customers.

If that language feels a little too secular, let's try to clarify the concept scripturally. Jesus said he came "to seek and to save what was lost"

(Luke 19:10). He commanded His followers to go into all the world and "make disciples" of those who were not followers (Matthew 28:19). One day Jesus pushed the concept to a radical extreme when he told the story about a shepherd who had a hundred sheep—He suggested that it was appropriate to abandon the ninety-nine that were safe in order to find the one that was lost.

WHEN TO IGNORE THE INSIDERS

What do you think Jesus would say about abandoning the almost 60 percent who presently attend church in America to reach the 40 percent who do not go? There is a massive potential audience being sacrificed because many churches are desperately trying to keep a handful of traditional customers satisfied.

The fact is you will rarely have to be intentional about listening to insiders in ministry. They will let you know what they think. Why? Because they're there! When is the last time you heard from those who do *not* come to your church? You don't hear from them because they're not there, and that's why you have to be deliberate if you want to know what they are thinking.

None of us can remember a time when someone who was unchurched called us to say, "I just wanted you to know that if you would do things different then I would start coming to your church." But we have endured countless phone calls and meetings with insiders who were frustrated or complaining when something didn't go their way.

Obviously, problems may arise if you choose to ignore your insiders for the sake of reaching outsiders. What if you lose some of the insiders? Chances are, you will, especially if the insiders are used to having their church world revolve around *them*. Some church leaders will warn against "sacrificing discipleship" for an approach that is "too

evangelistic" (as if it were possible to be too evangelistic). Others will
caution you about making a careful transition to this new emphasis in
order to get everyone on board (as if everyone will get on board).

We're not suggesting imbalance, nor are we suggesting you be care-
less. You should lead your church to invest in outsiders strategically.
You should strive to find the delicate balance between facilitating the
growth of believers and reaching those who are unchurched. But don't
make the mistake of piling up excuses and saddling your ministry with
an insider mindset that paralyzes your potential to reach outsiders. Too
many churches are hiding behind what is convenient and comfortable
while an entire generation is being left in the dark.

Any church with any history at all wrestles with becoming an
insider-minded organization. During the early days of North Point a
handful of frustrated members threatened to leave because we were not
accommodating their specific needs. The easy decision would have
been to accommodate them, to start whatever program we needed to
make them happy. But what Andy said to me that day has to be liber-
ating for anyone in ministry with a passion to reach outsiders. He said,
"This decision can't be based on who we will keep, but who we will
reach."

LISTEN TO INSIDERS WHO LISTEN TO OUTSIDERS

During one of our Monday morning meetings, we were struggling to
clarify our values as an organization. A defining moment happened
when a critical question was put on the table: "What would be something that if it ceased to be true about us as a church would make us
want to quit and go work somewhere else?" Every one of us admitted
we would quit if our church became so saturated with believers that
there was no room to reach outsiders.

The glue that has held our leadership team together through countless debates is an uncompromising commitment to create environments that will appeal to the unchurched. We strive to make North Point not only a safe place for outsiders, but also a safe place for insiders to bring outsiders—a place for believers to bring their unchurched friends

During the first year of our existence we crafted the phrase "invest and invite" as a way to challenge every leader and attendee to make outsiders their priority. This simple statement suggests that every person is responsible to make a personal investment in someone's life and bring them to one of North Point's environments. The concept has been contagious with everyone from leaders and elders to staff and attendees. We even know of some unbelievers who have invested and invited other outsiders!

When an insider invests in someone outside the church, something changes. The heart follows the investment, and the result is an authentic relationship between an insider and an outsider. That's why Jesus said, "Where your treasure is, there your heart will be also" (Matthew 6:21). What we have seen happen in the hearts of insiders has been just as significant as what we have witnessed in the hearts of outsiders. The "invest and invite" strategy has affected our church in a number of ways.

The "invest and invite" strategy has radically changed our approach to evangelism. Many of us grew up in churches that taught evangelism classes, gave altar calls, handed out tracts, and sent members to knock on the doors of strangers. However, none of these approaches effectively mobilized the majority of members to become personally involved in reaching the unchurched. To the average believer, most of these techniques seemed too confrontational or awkward. And so the responsibility for evangelism was usually assumed by a handful of trained "experts."

Later, many churches shifted toward a more natural approach, giving rise to a movement known as "lifestyle evangelism," or relational evangelism. The idea was that everyone should reprioritize their friendships to make sure they were investing in someone who needed Christ. This encourages spiritual dialogue in a safe context of authentic friendship for both the insider and outsider. It's the opposite of the typical "car salesman" approach to evangelism. Lifestyle evangelism works in concert with the way relationships naturally happen, and it is something that almost every believer can do.

There is only one problem. This approach can come up short for a number of reasons. For example, every believer speaks from a different level of spiritual maturity. What do you do when you have taken a friend as far as you can? Where does your friend go then? How do you explain issues you may not feel equipped to explain? That's why we say "invest and invite." The *invite* allows the believer to bring a friend into an environment where such issues can be addressed. Our Foyer and Kitchen environments are designed to be non-threatening, comfortable places to help unchurched friends move to the next step in their spiritual journey.

Of course, if we encourage attendees to practice investing without creating an effective environment where they can invite someone, the entire concept will break down. The majority of believers feel inadequate to evangelize their friends if they don't feel like the church will provide support when the questions become too complicated for the average believer to answer. When both sides of the "invest and invite" principle are practiced fervently, then everyone does what everyone does best. Believers become passionate about sharing their faith with friends, and staff members devote themselves to crafting environments where unchurched friends will feel welcomed and cared for.

FORMAL OR INFORMAL INVITATION?

From North Point's Playbook

A leader from another church who visited our services asked, "Why aren't you evangelistic?" It was surprising to us that he had attended a number of our environments and yet wondered about our passion to reach outsiders. He said, "I noticed that at the end of your service you did not give a formal invitation."

For many, evangelism is defined as giving an altar call of some kind at the end of every service. It makes sense. If you're priority is to reach outsiders, then why would you pass up an opportunity for them to respond to the gospel? On the other hand, we have discovered that a *formal* invitation has the potential to become a barrier for some people.

We challenged the same church leader with some questions of our own: "Should we assume that everyone who comes into our church, regardless of their background, is okay with the idea of standing up and pushing their way past a group of strangers? Do you think it's necessary for someone to go in front of several thousand people and have a discussion with someone they have never met about what they think is a very personal issue?"

Don't misunderstand. We're not suggesting that kind of invitation is wrong. And certainly it is important to help everyone know how to take the next step to become a Christian. But we believe that our "invest and invite" strategy is helping many of our members to give friends a more personal *informal* invitation every Sunday. And we are convinced by the stories and testimonies from the number of people who trust Christ each week that a formal invitation should not be a weekly part of our particular culture.

Every church has to discover what works in their culture to help outsiders take the important step to becoming a Christian. But chances are, if our staff showed up at a church that did a formal invitation each week where outsiders were coerced to take that long walk before they could become a Christian, we might be tempted to ask that church, "Why aren't you evangelistic? Why do you make it so difficult for someone to trust Christ, when the Bible makes it so simple?"

The "invest and invite" strategy inspires everyone to listen more attentively to what an outsider hears. When outsiders are invited to attend and they actually show up, everything changes. Imagine this scenario. You have worked side by side with an associate for a number of years. You have invested in his life. You spend quality time with him and his family. You have proven to be a trusted friend in his life, and you have encouraged him for several months to visit your church. At the end of your workday one Friday, he announces to you that he is planning to bring his family to visit your church that Sunday. How does that make you feel? Do you begin to wonder about what the church is planning for Sunday? You may even be tempted to call and see who is speaking or what the topic is—just to be sure that everything is going to be just right. How will it affect you as you sit next to him during the service? The fact is, that day will be different for you than a typical Sunday. You will hear everything differently as you try to imagine how your friend is hearing what is being said. You will be listening through the ears of an outsider.

When enough people show up with friends on a consistent basis, everyone in your church will be forced to listen through an entirely different filter. Everything your church does will be evaluated by a much more critical standard. We have discovered that inviting outsiders effectively keeps us aware and sensitive to how they think and what they need. If we drop the ball on any given Sunday, it is not uncommon for us to get a flood of e-mails with suggestions on how we can improve. People want their friends to have a good first impression of the church.

It puts healthy pressure on us to consider carefully how we program and communicate. That doesn't mean we water down the truth of what we teach, but we are keenly aware of *how* we say what we say. Andy, for example, is careful when approaching an issue that he knows is going to be awkward for outsiders to handle. Sometimes it is as simple as Andy acknowledging that we understand that they may think our perspective seems illogical or narrow. Sometime that's just the nature of the truth we teach. The worst thing to do would be to simply teach the insiders as if outsiders were not in the room. Then we would be guilty of ignoring and even being rude to our guests.

When attendees and volunteers are accustomed to having the unchurched or unbelievers in attendance, they cannot help but recognize the significance of how they act and serve. We have seen members give up seats for visitors, and in many cases attend an earlier, less crowded service to make more room for outsiders. When KidStuf became so crowded that some families couldn't get in, there were actually parents who stopped coming just so unchurched families could participate. From the parking lot to the nursery, everyone seems to be aware of and committed to making outsiders feel at home.

To put it another way, our insiders have decided that the needs of outsiders are more important than their own. When that happens the "listen to outsiders" practice has become an integral part of your culture.

Our leadership team has recently debated the question, "Who is our customer?" At one level, we all agree that our primary customer is the outsider who is not attending. But we have also admitted that the best way to listen to outsiders is to listen to the insiders who are outsider-minded. If their hearts are really focused on the needs and issues that outsiders face, then what they have to say to us is critical.

LISTEN TO ORGANIZATIONS THAT ARE REACHING OUTSIDERS

Years ago, Tony Campolo wrote a book with the intriguing title *We Have Met the Enemy and They Are Partly Right*. In it, Campolo implied that Christians could learn a lot from organizations that are not Christian. It makes sense that if we are targeting a certain age group or demographic we need to study the experts in our culture that have proven most effective at reaching that group. For example our children's ministries keep an eye on the Disney Channel, Nickelodeon, the Cartoon Network, etc. Our student ministry will learn from MTV and the WB network when it comes to identifying student issues. Recently, when Andy worked on his series for men and women in business, we brought in numerous back issues of *Fast Company* magazine and covered a creative board with articles that addressed issues the business community was currently facing.

Billions of dollars are spent every year by organizations in order to learn about and market to the same outsiders we are trying to reach. In a number of instances, when we thought we intuitively understood the issues, we found out we were wrong. Again, many of us have been inside so long, we have become deaf to what outsiders say their real needs are. If you are deaf long enough, it affects the way you speak. The reason a lot of churches are not connecting to outsiders is that they just haven't spent enough time learning the right language.

To effectively listen to outsiders, you must learn their language.

SPEAKING THE RIGHT LANGUAGE

Years ago I attended a denominational pastor's conference where Bill Hybels had been invited to speak. It was extremely rare for someone outside the denomination to speak, and there was some controversy over the event, as a number of pastors questioned the decision to give Hybels the platform. For one thing, some denominational leaders quibbled over the use of drama, secular music, and other techniques that Willow Creek had implemented to effectively reach outsiders.

The next day there was tension in the air when Bill Hybels stepped onto the platform. Following a challenging performance by Willow Creek's drama team, Hybels focused on an illustration of Jesus attending a party at Matthew's house. Throughout the hour he crafted a classic message about having a heart to "seek and save the lost." I was strategically positioned behind one of the denomination's prominent leaders, eagerly waiting to hear his response to what Hybels had to say. Halfway through the message, he leaned over to one of the younger pastors and remarked, "I don't see what all the fuss is about. He doesn't sound like a preacher at all. He speaks more like a layman."

I remember thinking, *You've been listening through the ears of a preacher for so long, you can't hear what you need to hear. You're missing it. You are evaluating his preaching technique instead of listening to what he is saying.*

Besides, isn't that the point? Bill Hybels *should* speak like a layman.

He is passionate about speaking the language of the people he is trying to reach, and that's why he is reaching thousands of seekers every week.

That was more than a decade ago, and it's sad to think there are still leaders who just don't get it. Bill Hybels has been a pioneer in rethinking a church's role in reaching the culture. Most leaders who heard Hybels that day went back to business as usual in churches with declining attendance. But there were some who became dissatisfied with simply nurturing and reaching insiders and were inspired to change the way they do church.

THE DAY AMERICA WENT TO CHURCH

The Sunday following September 11, 2001, should be etched in every church leader's mind forever. Our world had been rocked by one of the greatest tragedies in American history, and it is interesting to note where the majority of our population turned during the crisis. The average American, who was generally disinterested in matters of faith, showed up at their local church that Sunday.

At North Point, the building was jammed with outsiders. People were on edge and they needed spiritual direction. Late that night I was at home with one of my teenage daughters watching the news. A major network had documented what happened that day at churches across the country. We sat and watched footage of thousands of people lining up outside synagogues, cathedrals, and churches. We listened to sound bites and excerpts from priests, rabbis, and pastors as they addressed the public at this critical moment in our nation's history. But that night we both listened with different ears.

When the program ended my daughter said, "It's so sad."

"What do you mean?" I asked.

"That all those people went to church and it doesn't seem like anyone said what they needed to hear."

Then she said, "I just really wish they had heard what I heard today."

The next week the crowds dwindled, and most churches went back to their routines.

What if we decided every Sunday had the potential to be like that Sunday following September 11? What if we spent every week getting ready for a host of outsiders who could possibly show up? When you listen to outsiders, it forces you to change the way you do church.

IMPROVING YOUR GAME

- List the environments outside of your organization where you regularly interact with unchurched people.

- In what areas should your organization carefully guard against the tendency of catering to the insiders?

- Which environments in your organization have been specifically designed with outsiders in mind?

- Who are the "outside" experts reaching your target audience?

15

REPLACE YOURSELF

Learn to hand off what you do

I started collecting baseball cards as a kid in the late 1960s and early '70s. These fragile bits of cardboard bearing the images and statistics of players like Johnny Bench, Reggie Jackson, and Hank Aaron are still among my most prized possessions. These guys were legends in their own time.

I will always remember April 8, 1974. I was fourteen years old, and I can still see the image of one man swinging a bat. It was a magical night when Hammerin' Hank Aaron walloped home run number 715 and trotted around the bases, past Babe Ruth's longtime record and into history. I thought about that night again in 1998 when, with one swing, Mark McGwire shattered Roger Maris's thirty-one-year-old record for most home runs in a season. Watching McGwire round the bases, I thought, *No matter who you are, how famous or powerful, one day somebody will replace you.*

Shortly after President George H. W. Bush left office, our staff attended a conference where Bush was the keynote speaker. He described in detail his final flight on Air Force One after the inauguration of Bill Clinton. That day Bush woke up in the White House and went to bed in a rented house in Houston. He said that the next morning he woke up early and started reaching around in the dark, trying to find the button that for years had signaled the staff that he wanted a cup of coffee. He accidentally woke up Barbara, who figured out what he was trying to do. She said, "George, you're just going to have to get up and go get it yourself. It's over!"

It's sobering but unavoidable. One day it will be over. One day someone else will be doing what you are doing. One day you will be replaced. Whether you have an exit strategy or not, you *will* ultimately exit. And on that day, everything you've done, everything you've dreamed, and everything you've built will be placed in someone else's hands.

Like everyone else, you're probably planning on making your mark and leaving a legacy. But if you're anything like me, you tend to make plans with tomorrow in mind, not the next decade. And although deep down you know one day you will no longer be in the picture, nothing in the way you work or live testifies that you've really embraced the idea.

The fact is, you have only one of two choices:

1. You can desperately hold on to your job until someone inevitably replaces you.
2. You can prepare someone to do what you do and strategically replace yourself.

The first option gives you limited input in what happens in the future of your organization; the second allows you to leverage your influence with the next generation who will one day lead your organization. When you attempt to hold on, you encourage your organization to be built around a personality; when you strategically replace yourself, you allow your organization to be driven by a *vision*. Learning to effectively hand off leadership to the next generation is vital to the longevity of any organization, especially the church.

STUDENT IMPACT
From North Point's Playbook

If apprenticing volunteers is the best way to disciple and develop adults, why shouldn't the same approach work with teenagers? So we developed Student Impact to put teenagers on the front lines of our ministry environments. Some churches object, but when we honestly listened to our students, we learned that most of them don't want to be stuck in a room on Sunday morning. Instead, we have them serving on the mission field.

When Student Impact teams became involved in our Waumba Land, UpStreet, KidStuf, and Extreme ministries, the benefits were immediate. Suddenly, our kids were experiencing servant leadership. The middle school students were being mentored by an age group they respected, and our elementary school kids saw that serving others was a way to be "cool." And the high school kids had a reason to be there on Sunday mornings!

True discipleship is about serving and being involved. Our students are not just hearing about distant ideas; they are part of a revolution. Our high school program is now scheduled for Sunday afternoons so teens can serve in the morning programs. Every week, students at North Point go to work changing diapers, aiding teachers, leading worship music, and serving families. They change lives, and in doing so, they are changed.

TEAR DOWN LEADERSHIP WALLS

Several years ago John Maxwell introduced our staff to the concept of "leadership lids." A lid is anything that keeps a leader from growing. Maxwell explained that there are certain aspects of your personality that can prevent you from achieving your full potential; therefore, it is important for leaders to identify their lids and do whatever they can to lift them. An organization will have a difficult time rising higher than the lid of its leader.

We've discovered that organizations also have "leadership walls" that prevent *others* from achieving *their* potential. Whereas a leadership lid can stunt your personal growth as a leader and may indirectly affect the rest of your organization, a leadership wall can directly stunt the growth of those on your team and, ultimately, create a leadership gap in your organization. Lids may stop leaders from growing up, but walls keep leaders out. They form a barrier that blocks the development of future leaders in your organization.

If you fail to develop a strategy to replace yourself, you will...
> **...force talented individuals to remain in the wings.**
> **...cause potential leaders to exit the organization.**
> **...stifle needed insight from valuable team members.**
> **...hinder your ability to recruit volunteers.**
> **...limit the growth of your programs and ministries.**

Every leader needs to take an honest, objective look at anything that may create a barrier to the growth of the church's staff and volunteers. Consider this possibility: The same characteristics that make a leader effective may also adversely affect his or her ability to reproduce other leaders. Here are a few examples of how different leader's attributes can actually build leadership walls that hinder the development of future leaders.

The *entrepreneurial* leader specializes in taking risks and pioneering new territory, yet may see others' fresh ideas as threatening or in competition with his own.

The *nurturing* leader is patient and encouraging, but may lack the zeal to confront someone in areas that really need to change.

The *charismatic* leader can inspire the masses to follow a dream, yet may become jealous and defensive when the time comes for people to follow a new leader.

The *innovative* leader uses creativity to produce something relevant and original, but tends to get possessive when another artist tries to improve on what has been created.

The *managing* leader is excellent at coordinating staff and developing systems, yet may stubbornly resist those who question the process or want to experiment with doing things in a different way.

The *high-performance* leader can juggle an incredible workload and still be extremely productive, but his failure to delegate does not allow anyone else to really own a piece of the vision.

Replacing yourself begins with a shift in your thinking as a leader. It demands that you face some personal tendencies that could be unhealthy for your organization. The signs are more obvious than you might think: The pastor insists on being the only speaker; administrators are easily frustrated by suggestions; progress is slow because only a few people are allowed to make decisions; the same singers or musicians are featured every week; staff members routinely stay late because they think they're the only ones who can do a job; raises and bonuses reflect only personal productivity.

As a leader, you have probably been taught to focus on what makes you a strong leader. We agree. We are passionate about the idea of "playing in your zone." But not to the point of being a ball hog at the expense of your team. You also need to focus on what makes other leaders strong. This may require you to concentrate at times on the areas that make it difficult for you to replace yourself as a leader. Instead of asking the question, "What keeps *me* from growing as a leader?" you should spend more time asking, "What keeps *those around me* from growing as leaders?"

APPLAUD THOSE WHO APPLAUD OTHERS

Replacing yourself means that you are willing to hand someone else a significant piece of what you do. You are then responsible to help this person own it and succeed at it. When he or she succeeds, make sure they are applauded and recognized for what they have done. And be ready to applaud those leaders who applaud someone else who has effectively done their job. When you applaud leaders who push others into the spotlight, you send a message to everyone about what is really important in your organization.

Most leaders are complimented and compensated according to their ability to innovate, create, produce, manage, and perform. The reason they don't practice replacing themselves is because it is rarely applauded. No wonder leaders are so focused on their own personal development instead of developing others! Whenever a leader tries to build job security by making himself indispensable to the organization, he in fact does the organization a disservice. Job security is too often based on someone's insecurity.

The practice of "replacing yourself" is critical to the longevity of any organization, but if you want the practice to become a habit in your church, you must recognize and reward it when it happens. Then every leader at every level needs to start celebrating it whenever they see leaders making other leaders successful.

POSITION YOUR VOLUNTEERS TO RECRUIT

We have explained why replacing yourself is important in the context of leaders who will one day exit your organization; it is also critical to see how this principle applies to expanding your base of volunteers. We consider our volunteer force to be our most critical resource. They hold the keys to the fulfillment of our vision for leading people into a growing relationship with Christ.

Some churches buy into the myth that it is the responsibility of a few staff to do most of the recruiting. When you embrace that mindset you immediately limit the number of volunteers you can scout and train. But if you can successfully inspire your existing volunteers to replace themselves, volunteerism has the opportunity to grow exponentially. The grassroots goal is to make sure that every volunteer makes it their mission to recruit another volunteer. Impossible? Maybe. But what if only half of your volunteers successfully found another person to do what they do? What if only one out of every four took up the challenge to replace themselves and they found someone new every several months? What kind of difference would that make in the growth of your volunteer base?

One distinction that separates the church from most other businesses is that it requires a significant number of volunteers to make it work. A small group model, for example, requires a leader for every ten to twelve individuals. The average company could never afford to hire someone to be exclusively devoted to only twelve customers. Within our family ministry alone, it takes more than thirteen hundred volunteers to make our weekly environments happen. At an average of two to three hours per volunteer, they collectively spend three thousand hours a week. If we were paying these people just ten dollars an hour, the price tag would be $30,000 each week.

Now consider that many of these people are highly skilled, and their value soars. Walk through our halls on a Sunday morning and you may meet a doctor who is video directing, a software developer running our computer graphics, a bank executive leading a small group of second graders, and a high school principal working with middle school students. Even if we could figure out how to pay for the number of hours these individuals collectively invest, we could *never* afford their level of expertise.

When we started North Point, we had only a few staff coordinating a number of ministries. We were trying to find volunteers, and because everyone was new, we had limited relationships with those who were attending. We would walk into meetings with a handful of volunteers and start handing out index cards. We would ask everyone to write down the name of two or three friends who could do what they do. Then we would challenge them to recruit at least one. At the next meeting everyone would give a report. We were surprised at how many actually came back with new volunteers!

A simple announcement or church bulletin insert is rarely successful in finding volunteers. Why? Because leaders don't volunteer; they are recruited. They respond to a personal invitation, not a general announcement. One of the reasons we keep getting great volunteers is that we have volunteers who replace themselves.

TEACH WHAT YOU KNOW

The most effective way to train people is to model what needs to be done by apprenticing, but this can be a frightening idea for the average leader. Certain myths exist that cloud what apprenticing really means. For example, one notion is that you must be more skilled than the person you are apprenticing. However, you are not responsible for knowing *everything* there is to know about an area of ministry. But you *are* responsible for handing off what you *do* know. You don't have to be an incredibly talented player to coach someone how to become better at playing the game.

A few years ago *Fast Company* magazine profiled Doug Blevins, a man who had aspired all of his life to be an NFL football coach. So he started blitzing New York Jets manager Dick Steinberg with faxes detailing the flaws of Cary Blanchard, the Jets' place kicker at the time. Steinberg was evidently impressed with Blevins's knowledge of the game and hired him as a kicking consultant in 1994. The amazing thing is that Blevins himself has never attempted a field goal. He's never punted for any team, on any level, let alone in the NFL. Because he was born with cerebral palsy, he has, in fact, never even walked.[1]

The point is that you should not let what you don't know keep you from apprenticing someone. Your responsibility is to teach what you do know. And if you develop a heart to coach, you can help people grow and improve their skills.

REPLACEMENT ON A LARGER SCALE
From North Point's Playbook

After five years of growth had maxed out our present facility, we had to do something, and it soon became evident that God's plan for North Point involved a multi-campus strategy where we would establish similar models of ministry in strategic locations. Through the leadership of David McDaniel, our director of campus expansion, these campuses would provide relief from overcrowding and offer to each new location a relevant church model.

From the beginning our leadership team has promoted a franchise mindset that insists we intentionally replace ourselves. And so we had already established systems of ministry as well as qualified personnel to staff these new campuses. This approach allowed key staff members from our Alpharetta campus to move to the new campuses because there were structures and people in place to replace them.

As God blesses your ministry, you may have to duplicate yourself as often as you replace yourself.

THREE STEPS TO HANDING IT OFF

Reproducing more leaders to do more of the same things is the only way we can consistently meet the growing demands of more small groups, more productions, and more campuses. And it has been key to our developing specialized talent.

The following are three steps to making a successful hand-off.

1. Break It Down

Teaching someone to replace you begins by having a clear understanding of exactly what it is you are trying to hand off. *Fast Company* made this observation about Doug Blevins, "Trainers in every business can learn from Blevins's teaching techniques. He breaks each motion down to its component parts, then squeezes out incremental but critical improvements. And he knows just how much he can change in a player—and when he should leave well enough alone."[2]

If you are going to apprentice someone to do what you do, then you need to know what it *is* you do. Because if you can't explain or define what you do, then it will be hard to get someone else to do it.

Each function must be broken down into clear and doable steps and possibly even scripted. Chances are if it is not written down, then it has probably not been effectively broken down. There is something about going through the process of putting a task on paper and breaking it down into steps that makes it easier to transfer to someone else.

On the other hand, what you do may be so intuitive that it's difficult to articulate or teach. For example, Andy is a gifted communicator, and there is just something about the way he prepares, studies, creates, outlines, and speaks that is hard for him to explain. So how does Andy transfer to someone else what he knows how to do intuitively? How can he use his knowledge to train other communicators to become more effective? To help, we actually have spent time studying what Andy does and scripting his moves. Lane is actively watching his techniques and recording his processes. Why? So he can break it down in a way that someone else can repeat.

2. Hand It Off

When replacing yourself, you are giving something away that you have owned. You are equipping someone to do something that you have done, pushing them into a role that you have played. Assuming you are human, you will likely experience a jumble of emotions during the hand-off. And if the ball is dropped, you will tend to want to pick it back up quickly. But remember, you are training someone else to carry the ball. Don't try to be the hero who recovers the fumble and carries it across the goal line himself. You're there to coach and model. Everyone learns best from mistakes, so allow others to learn from theirs. Your job is to help push someone else across the goal line for the score.

People who embrace the "replace yourself" principle see others around them as partners, not competition. In our Family Ministry division, every volunteer undergoes an initial screening process through general orientation before being assigned to a leader who will then connect with them and model the specific skill they are learning. First, this allows us to observe and assess each volunteer in an apprentice role. Second, it gives people the confidence to serve effectively. Again, most people want to win, and apprenticing gives them an opportunity to learn *how* to win before they are called upon to play in the game on their own.

Meanwhile, as apprentices learn and develop new skills, you will be sharpening your ability to apprentice others. You may practice apprenticing for years before you have to apprentice someone to actually take your place. But that day will come. And what you do now can prepare you for what you will have to do later. Now it is important for individuals in your church to learn the skill of handing off. The day will come when it will be crucial for those individuals to let go.

3. Let It Go

This will be hard, but necessary. Sooner or later, you will have to let go, so start practicing now. God gives us various opportunities throughout our life to learn this lesson. We leave home as college students. We watch our kids become independent. We lose someone whom we love. Life keeps moving, and there are times when we have to just let go. It is usually difficult. It always requires trust. But our understanding of the bigger picture gives us the wisdom to let go and transition to whatever's next.

An unexpected merger happened a few years ago when Larry Burkett, founder of Christian Financial Concepts, determined that it was time for him let go of his leadership and merge his nonprofit organization with another entity. This would mean that Burkett would allow others to leverage what he had spent twenty-five years building. The partner he chose was one that some might have considered to be his competition, Crown Ministries. But what Burkett modeled as he worked through that transition is an incredible lesson for Christian leaders.

On one occasion he was quoted as saying, "My greatest fear in life is standing before the Lord and hearing him say, 'I had so much more for you, but you held on too tightly.'" Larry Burkett recognized something that is just too easy for so many of us to miss: It's easier to let go of what doesn't belong to you anyway. When you are focused on the scope of God's kingdom, you realize there is something more important than your personal dream or agenda. Burkett recognized that there was greater potential to reach others if he combined his efforts with Crown Ministries than if he remained independent. That decision stands as a clear illustration of the power of letting go in the right way.

Those closest to Burkett claim that the decision to merge was really just one in a series of decisions that reflected a life characterized by kingdom-mindedness. Consider some of the following examples.

Burkett gave away the two million dollars he had earned from selling his personal business prior to starting his ministry. When asked why he didn't save some of it for his nonprofit endeavor, Burkett said that he wanted to depend on God to meet his needs.

At one time there had been an opportunity to sue another Christian over a matter of plagiarism for a significant amount of money. Burkett refused, saying that they were God's ideas anyway, and maybe the materials would reach more people.

In 1982 he helped to start the National Christian Foundation, which later had an opportunity to merge with a handful of other foundations. Others pointed out the possibility that they could cover the country and control everything. He rejected the idea of building to gain control, but he liked the idea of covering the country. So instead, Burkett influenced the board of NCF to focus on helping various communities start smaller foundations to serve specific regions.

When someone suggested that Crown Ministry was his "biggest competitor," Larry became indignant. "There is no competition in the Christian world," he said. He then proceeded to invite Crown Ministry's

Howard Dayton to be interviewed on his radio broadcast to promote the "competing" ministry.

Larry Burkett had a habit of giving away what he had.

He believed that God's agenda was more important than his own.

Those who knew him say he held everything with an open hand.

So it's no surprise that when it came time, it was easy for him to let go.

He had had years of practice.

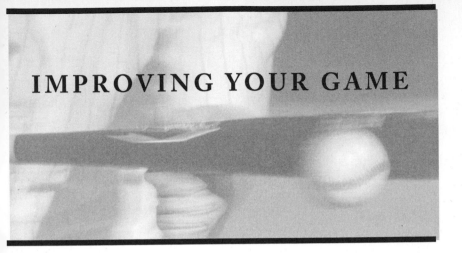

IMPROVING YOUR GAME

- Identify the leaders in your organization. What is your plan for replacing these leaders?

- Who are you personally investing in to do *your* job after you're gone?

- Which reproducible systems are now in place in your organization that will make it easy to transfer responsibilities to others?

- Which of the leadership types listed on page 161 do you most identify with? Do you also identify with the potential weaknesses listed for this type of leader?

- Which of the unhealthy personal tendencies listed on page 161 can your team identify with?

practice #7

WORK ON IT

Take time to evaluate your work—
and to celebrate your wins

Baseball's annual spring training is a reminder that even the best in the game need a time of focused training and practice. All you have to do is watch one spring training game and you realize that the fundamentals tend to break down with even the best players if they don't work on their skills. That's why Barry Bonds has a batting coach. Think about it. Arguably the best hitter in the game today, and one of the best of all time, Bonds turns to *someone else* to help him analyze his swing. Bonds recognizes that it isn't enough to play the game—you have to work on your game, too.

Those of us who work in ministry are no different. No matter how long we've served, no matter how many sermons we've preached, no matter how many successful ministries we've launched—if we are not consistently evaluating both our performance and our strategies, at some point we will begin to swing and miss.

Self-evaluation is not a new concept. The book of Genesis records that God set aside a time for evaluating His own work. At the end of six long days of creating, Scripture tells us that before He rested, He evaluated. He saw all that He had made and, behold, "it was very good" (Genesis 1:31). Now God obviously had an advantage in that all He creates is good and so the evaluation probably didn't take too long. But He looked at it nonetheless. Later we learn that He evaluated Adam's situation and saw that it was not good for man to be alone, and we are all grateful that God took the time to work on the system that day.

The point is, no matter how good the system, a consistent time of evaluation can produce tremendous benefits. We call this *creating margin*. Andy has challenged us, as a staff as well as personally, to create margin in our lives. Margin does not happen accidentally, and it doesn't happen automatically. Margin has to be pursued.

BUILDING MARGIN INTO THE CALENDAR

For most of us, our margin is what's left over after we've finished doing everything we have to do. It's an afterthought. But for margin to be effective, it has to be an integral part of your overall plan. At the outset, you have to schedule consistent times to break away from the battle and assess your plan as well as your performance. No matter how hard you try, it simply can't be done as you go.

I worked for a few years in a church that was so large we had painters on staff. The paint crew would start at one end of the campus, and by the time they completed every room in the church, it was time to start over. I'll never forget the day they painted my office. I walked in that morning to the most noxious fumes I ever encountered. I elected to duck into my office and grab a few things before beating a hasty retreat. While there I asked one of the painters how he could stand to work around the fumes. "What fumes?" he said.

Sometimes it's hard to smell something if you're surrounded by it every day. It's like coming home after a week's vacation—when you walk in the door, you recognize an odor that had become so familiar, you had stopped smelling it. You can't evaluate something if you stay in the middle of it too long. You can't help but miss some things. Things you've seen for so long that you just don't see them anymore. Things that have started to decay and you've become accustomed to the smell.

This is why we have carved time out of our schedule that is not given to the daily routine of working in ministry. We place a high premium on retreats and off-site meetings where our staff can get away, step back, and take a big-picture view of things.

TIME TO ACT LIKE THEN IS NOW
From North Point's Playbook

One of the important things we learned early on was that if we were ever going to be a big church that made a big impact, we would have to start acting like one even before we were. We started doing leadership team planning retreats, even when the leadership team was practically the entire staff. It wasn't that we needed to get away from everyone because *we were* everyone. But we knew that one day we wouldn't be. And so we established an annual off-site event where we celebrated what had happened the previous year and planned for the next.

At one of the first of these off-site events, Andy challenged the six of us to develop a staff organizational chart for a church of five thousand people. This was when our congregation was a fraction of that number. But we designed the chart and inserted our staff's names in every box. This gave us a blueprint to grow by. And as we grew, we slowly replaced our names with the amazing team that we have today. Once we reached five thousand in attendance, you can guess what the focus of the retreat was that year—a chart for a church of ten thousand.

WEEKLY STORY TIME

At North Point, we have made evaluation a part of our weekly routine. Every Monday morning, the seven members of our leadership team get together to "work on it." The value of this meeting is difficult to overstate. In addition to discussing the issues and opportunities that present themselves each week, we are able to share firsthand the successes and failures that occur in each of our areas, as well as give input and insight into other areas. The relational value of this meeting alone makes it worth the time as we speak into one another's lives. We also include other church staff in this meeting in order to expose them to the ideas and dynamics of the leadership team.

Monday is also the day we meet as a staff—the entire staff, which is getting pretty big now—at which time Andy asks everyone the same question: "What did you see, hear, or experience this week that makes you feel we have successfully fulfilled our mission?" The stories we share in response tell us that we have successfully "worked on it"; we recognize that when the stories stop coming, it means we are no longer being effective.

Additionally, every one of our creative meetings where we plan an environment includes an evaluation phase when we look at our effectiveness in the previous week. During our worship service evaluation time, we perform an intensive autopsy of the service, ensuring that we can repeat those things that worked and hopefully avoid repeating the ones that didn't. These small but specific times of evaluation are critical pieces of margin that have been created and are carefully guarded.

Calendaring margin goes beyond scheduling a specific time for evaluation. It may also involve stopping a program or activity for a strategic period of time. For example, attendance at many of our programs slows considerably or stops altogether during the summer months. This gives our leadership extended time to evaluate the programs and often realign them. Just like a car, a ministry can easily get out of alignment. These subtle shifts of direction are difficult to see when you're heading down the road at top speed; but by scheduling an extended downtime, the leadership can put the ministry up on the rack and check it out thoroughly. These downtimes also provide a much-needed break for a huge number of volunteers—it's far easier to go into the fall all fired up when you've had the summer to recuperate.

Another example of calendaring margin is the unheard-of decision by our elders to cancel services on the Sunday following Christmas. On that Sunday we simply shut down. We do this for two reasons: first, as a thank-you to the thousands of volunteers it takes to run a Sunday morning here; and second, to protect the quality of our product. So many of our volunteers travel on that weekend that we find it difficult to maintain the level of excellence to which we are accustomed. But by scheduling this closure and announcing it to everyone, we are able to take a potentially negative situation and turn it into a positive one.

We have discovered that in these moments of created margin, we get some of our best ideas. We are able to solve some of our most complex problems and refocus our energies in a way that makes a huge difference in our future ministry.

A LEARNING ORGANIZATION
From North Point's Playbook

In his book *The Fifth Discipline*, Peter Senge coined the term "the learning organization." One of the primary aspects of "working on it" is to continue to learn as an organization. Our leadership team, as well as some of the other ministry teams in the church, often read through business and leadership books as a group.

Nearly half the time in our Monday morning meetings is spent discussing the current book and its application to our circumstances. Here are some of the books we've read:

The E Myth by Michael Gerber
The Fifth Discipline by Peter Senge
Focus by Al Ries
Built to Last by Jim Collins
Good to Great by Jim Collins
The Five Temptations of a CEO by Patrick Lencioni
The Five Dysfunctions of a Team by Patrick Lencioni
The 80/20 Principle by Richard Koch
Paradigms by Joel Arthur Barber
What the Best CEOs Know by Jeffrey Krames
Courageous Leadership by Bill Hybels

Many of the seven practices in this book are direct applications of principles and ideas that have grown out of our leadership team book discussions.

CONFRONTING THE FACTS

There's nothing like a bad day on the field to produce good copy in the sports page the next day. It amazing how an honest evaluation can lead to some pretty ugly observations. Ideally, your organization will be much like Creation was when God took time to evaluate it. You will look at it and, behold, it is very good. Or you might end up like the rest of us, confronted with some not very pretty facts. The fact is that when people are involved, there are always areas that need improvement. Sometimes it's as simple as improving performance. I say "simple" because we have found that performance issues are easier to see and fix than are systems issues.

When you have carved out margin to work on a specific area, you have created an environment where you can turn over the rocks and confront what Jim Collins calls "the brutal facts."[1] During such times, everyone on our staff is encouraged to make suggestions and everyone takes suggestions. These are often times of intense dialogue and debate, and at times there are tears. There are no sacred cows or sacred programs. Everything is up for debate and must be defended against our mission and values. This is one of the ways we stay aligned with our purpose. At the end of the day, when the dust settles, we have asked the tough questions and hopefully arrived at the right answers.

A word of warning: Common sense tells us that open and honest debate creates the potential for negative impact on relationships. In order to keep your staff from paying the price relationally, you must develop an atmosphere of trust throughout your team. We use a word picture of each of us carrying two buckets at all times. One is full of water; the other is full of gasoline. When honest debate leads to a difference of opinion, it's a good thing. But when it leads to gossip and backbiting, it can be deadly. There needs to be a mutual commitment among the staff that all fires are to be doused with a bucket of water and not fed with a bucket of gasoline. If your staff will choose to trust one another and assume the best, you will have an atmosphere where debate can take its full and natural course without fear of retribution or reprisal.

CELEBRATING THE STORIES

A key thing to remember about creating margin in your organization is that it isn't enough to evaluate. You also have to celebrate. It never fails to move me when I see a baseball team celebrating a World Series victory. I am moved because in those moments of sheer joy are enfolded the story of thousands of hours of sacrifice, practice, and effort. The stories of millions of Little Leaguers fielding grounders and millions of fathers throwing thousands of batting practice pitches are expressed in those moments of unbridled celebration.

At North Point we not only evaluate our effectiveness by sharing stories, we share our stories to celebrate those involved. It is a unique chance for ministries to publicly acknowledge and thank their peers who've played a pivotal role in making a great story happen. We've seen many people from our facilities and administration areas moved to tears when they hear a "frontline" ministry share how their faithfulness in small things has resulted in a life being changed in a big way.

We have also made the celebration of stories a central part of our Sunday morning worship experience. Whenever someone comes to be baptized, we show a one- to two-minute video of that person telling his or her story. These people often take this opportunity to publicly thank those whom God has used to make a difference in their lives. We are then able to say to the congregation, many of whom are unbelievers, that these stories are why we do what we do.

If you want a behavior repeated then you need to reward it. Few things are more rewarding for a volunteer than hearing his or her name shared as part of someone's life-changing story.

A NIGHT TO REMEMBER
From North Point's Playbook

One of the biggest challenges we face is adequately and appropriately honoring a large number of volunteers. In our Family Ministry division, which encompasses thousands of volunteers working with everyone from preschool kids to married adults, we have solved this dilemma through our annual Strategic Service Awards.

This is an Academy Awards-like event where each ministry area hosts their volunteers for dinner and provides an entertaining show built around the work of the department. We spotlight certain workers through stories shared by children and adults in their area of ministry. The stories that these people share of how God has used the faithfulness of a particular volunteer to impact their lives are the highlight of the evening. All volunteers receive a special gift thanking them for their service.

This event is a large and expensive production, and purposely so. Our intention is to communicate the great value we place on our volunteers by giving them a night to remember.

A CRITICAL QUESTION

No one reading this book will ever have to ask if they're working *in* their ministry. That's what we do. The critical question that we all must ask is, Am I consistently carving out the time to work *on* the ministry? All great athletes watch film of their performance on the field. All great athletes spot problems and seek to correct them. And all great athletes celebrate their victories. If that much planning and effort is expended on a ring or a trophy, how much more should we expend to impact someone eternally?

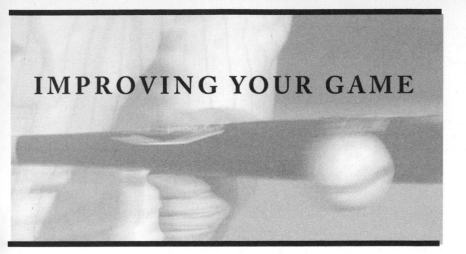

IMPROVING YOUR GAME

- Does your present meeting structure allow time for sharing learning experiences? What percentage of your meetings is spent simply downloading information?

- Discuss ways you can effectively encourage learning throughout your organization.

- How much of your time do you spend just working on what is happening in your weekly programming versus discussing overall strategy?

- Make a list of issues your team needs to discuss that don't directly impact what happens in your weekly programs—for example, how you reach outsiders, increasing small group participation, identifying what's not working, developing a hiring philosophy, etc.

- Would the members of your organization say that their contributions are valued and that time is taken to properly honor these contributions? In what areas and what ways could you improve in this area?

- Identify a specific win you could celebrate with your team. What would that celebration look like? Now put it on the calendar!

A FINAL
CHALLENGE

from Andy Stanley

Your ministry is perfectly designed to achieve the results you are currently getting. If you are satisfied with your results, then there is no sense in complicating your life with these seven practices. But if you are ready for change, if you see a need for improvement, then the principles in this book will give you traction as you press on toward your preferred future.

At North Point we have found that each of the practices anchor the organization to specific components of our mission and strategy. For example, *Clarify the Win* fuels our momentum. *Think Steps, Not Programs* protects our alignment. *Narrow the Focus* points us towards excellence. *Teach Less for More* guarantees that we stay relevant. *Listen to Outsiders* keeps us focused on growth. *Replace Yourself* assures us of longevity. And *Work On It* positions us for discovery.

Whether you have identified them or not, your organization has established some practices of its own. There are certain assumptions and rules that govern your decision-making processes. Every organization has them. You may not be able to articulate them all, but you know when you have bumped up against one: Somebody always reacts.

No doubt, some of your organization's practices have been challenged as you worked through these pages. So now what? What's your next move?

I suggest picking one, maybe two, of these practices and begin teaching them to your leadership. In addition, look for opportunities to model the principle you are highlighting. For example, find one unfocused environment and focus it. Preach a one-point message. Spend an entire planning session clarifying the win for one program. In other words, involve people in the process of discovering the value of these practices.

In addition, when you discover a current practice that needs to be abandoned, name it and then get your team to buy in to discarding it. For example, if instead of teaching less for more your communicators have a tendency to teach "until the time runs out," talk about it. Develop your own phrases to describe what should and shouldn't be done.

If your ministry has a history of leaders *entrenching* themselves rather than replacing themselves, talk about it. Contrast the two. Clarify what you are abandoning as well as what you are embracing.

If you will make these seven practices the grid through which you evaluate and plan, they will enable your ministry to emerge from the fog of misinformation and emotion that impede your progress.

I've always taken comfort in the fact that Jesus said *He* would build His church. I find this comforting because He promises to do the heavy lifting, while my responsibility as a local church leader is simply to keep in step with the Savior. Our prayer is that these practices will help you do just that.

NOTES

Chapter 11
1. *American Heritage Dictionary of the English Language: Fourth Edition,* 2000, s.v. "program."
2. *American Heritage Dictionary of the English Language: Fourth Edition,* 2000, s.v. "step."
3. Lewis Carroll, *Alice's Adventures in Wonderland*, in Martin Gardner, *The Annotated Alice* (New York: New American Library, 1960), 88.

Chapter 13
1. John Coné, quoted by Carol Dahle, "Learning—John Coné," *Fast Company*, December 1998, 178.
2. Malcolm Gladwell, *The Tipping Point: How Little Things Can Make a Big Difference* (Boston: Little, Brown, 2002).

Chapter 14
1. George Barna, *Grow Your Church from the Outside In: Understanding the Unchurched and How to Reach Them* (Ventura, CA: Regal Books, 2002), 23.

Chapter 15
1. Todd Shapera, "This Coach Helps the Best to Hit Their Stride," *Fast Company*, September 2000, 48.
2. Ibid.

Chapter 16
1. Jim Collins, *Good to Great* (New York: Harper Collins, 2001), 72.

"Andy Stanley offers a fresh perspective on ageless truths that will be of enormous benefit to today's leaders and to future generations."
— **Patrick S. Flood, chairman and CEO, HomeBanc Mortgage Corporation**

DON'T MISS THESE TITLES FROM ANDY STANLEY

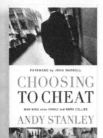

CHOOSING TO CHEAT

Choosing to Cheat presents a strategic plan for resolving the tension between work and home—reversing the destructive pattern of giving to your company and career what belongs to your family.

ISBN 1-59052-329-6

HOW GOOD IS GOOD ENOUGH?

Goodness is not even a requirement to enter God's kingdom—thankfully, because we'll never be good enough. And Christianity is beyond fair—it's merciful.

ISBN 1-59052-274-5

THE NEXT GENERATION LEADER

Be the kind of leader you'd admire! Find inspiration, encouragement, and proven advice from pastor and bestselling author Andy Stanley.

ISBN 1-59052-046-7

VISIONEERING

Andy Stanley shows readers how to set goals and obliterate the obstacles to a passionately-lived, meaningful life. He offers a workable plan for discovering a life vision aligned with God's own vision.

ISBN 1-57673-787-X

Available at Christian bookstores everywhere
www.bigchangemoments.com | www.multnomahbooks.com

Don't miss these additional ministry tools from Andy Stanley and Northpoint Resources!

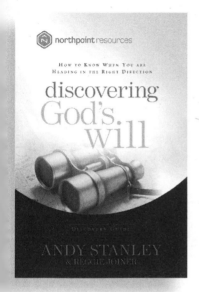

Discovering God's Will Study Guide

Designed for small groups or personal study, this companion study guide to the *Discovering God's Will* DVD will take readers through the important steps of decision making.

ISBN 1-59052-379-2

Parental Guidance Required Study Guide

This six-session companion study guide to the *Parental Guidance Required* DVD is a practical resource that will encourage parents to closely examine the relationships in their child's life.

ISBN 1-59052-381-4

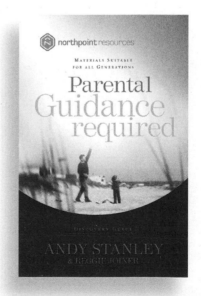